Tell Me The Tale

Historical Reflections on the Church of God

Tell Me The Tale

Historical Reflections on the Church of God

By Merle D. Strege

Warner Press, Inc.
Anderson, Indiana

Published by
Warner Press, Inc.
Anderson, Indiana

All scripture passages, unless otherwise indi-
cated, are from the King James Version or
the Revised Standard Version, © copyright
1972, Thomas Nelson.

Arlo F. Newell, Editor in Chief
Dan Harman, Book Editor
Cover by David Liverett

Other Warner Press books by Merle D.
Strege:
A Look at the Church of God for Children,
    Vol. I (1987).
A Look at the Church of God for Children,
    Vol. II (1989).

To my parents,
Ivan E. Strege
and
Joyce Wiuff Strege

Table of Contents

Introduction

I have written this book with a sincere hope for its usefulness among the people of the Church of God (Anderson, Indiana), of which I am a minister and academic servant. But I fully expect that it can and will be read for reasons other than those uppermost in my mind. There is nothing wrong with a book serving more than one purpose; in fact I would be delighted should that prove to be true of this one. By way of introduction, however, I wish to make a few comments about the way this book can be read and how I hope it might be used.

Someone who scans the contents page may wonder about this book's composition, for it seems to be a strange combination of stories and vignettes followed by three more or less technical theological and historical essays, the former resembling the latter not at all in either subject matter or tone. True enough, on one level the first and second parts of this book are quite disconnected. But their lack of connectedness is only apparent and not real.

This book does in fact bring together several stories from the history of the Church of God movement. Over several years I have become convinced of the importance of storytelling for the community called the church. The deep connection between our narratives and the communities of which we are parts is the subject of a growing body of literature.

This connection can be displayed in the Church of God movement as well. Additionally for us, however, narrative has been an important part of our life together in the form of the testimony, a feature of considerable historical significance in the Church of God way of being the church. A testimony is a story, told with the eye of faith, of what the Lord has done. Telling stories is an activity consonant with our own polity as well as the subject of recent theological scholarship.

Some of the people who pick up this volume will be attracted to the stories that comprise the first four chapters, and these people may have no real interest in the three concluding essays. If the stories published herein inspire or prompt readers to ask questions of themselves and the subjects of the stories, that will be a good outcome, and it is indeed one of my intentions for the use of this book.

Although the stories collected here may be entertaining, my purpose is not merely to amuse those who read them. The material gathered in Part One was chosen and arranged with a particular purpose. Chapters 5, 6, and 7 attempt to explain theologically that purpose. Thus the book *as a whole* is my effort to offer to the church an example of a kind of moral and theological reflection that I believe will serve the movement particularly well as it journeys on in the second century of its mission to the world and the still-divided body of Christ.

Some may wonder how a book of essentially historical reflections can pretend to be about theology and ethics. I have an answer to that question; it derives from three different and yet compatible definitions of theology. In *Pia Disideria*, Phillip Jakob Spener quoted a definition common among seventeenth-century Protestants: "Theology is a practical discipline" (Spener 1964:104-105). Spener was one of those earnest Christians whom we have come to label "Pietists," and his use of this common definition must be read as his effort to give everyday life a larger role in theology; in other words, he did not think theology was the private property of university professors. Thus the second definition of theology, offered by the German Lutheran pastor Johannes Arndt, fountainhead of the Pietist movement and the person Spener believed had rekindled the essence of Luther's thought and spirit: "Many think that theology is a mere science, or rhetoric, whereas it is a living experience and practice" (1979:21). The final definition of theology, more technical and detailed than the first two, comes from James McLendon, who says that theology is

> The discovery, understanding and transformation of the convictions of a convictional community, including their discovery and critical relation to one another *and to whatever else there is* (1986:23).

Each of these definitions has contributed much to my understanding, and displaying that understanding in the following set of statements should make clear why I offer this book as a theoretical and practical model of theological method.

(1) Theology is a *churchly* enterprise. Theology is an endeavor larger than the attempt to probe human experience from a religious point of view. Moreover, the theological audience must be regarded as larger than university campuses. Theologians work to discover, understand, and transform the deep commitments of the church. We discover those commitments in the formative narratives of our community. In those stories we begin to learn what kind of people we have been. In the same process we also learn something about our own character.

(2) Theology is a *historical* enterprise. Lived (and living) experience is the material out of which theology rises. Historical narrative is the attempt to reconstruct the lived experiences of the past. Thus, the historical narratives of the Christian community seem to be intimately connected to the work of theologians; indeed those narratives are part of that work. It may not be too much to say that the narratives of

the people of God already constitute a form of theological reflection.

(3) Theology is a *moral* enterprise. Particularly as it treats the moral convictions of the church, theology must be seen to have an interest in the kind of people the church is becoming. Like other groups who have emphasized the ideal of a holy life, the commitments of the Church of God have an especially deep stake in the moral conception of the Christian life. Hence, theology is not only what we think; it also is the manner in which our lives express that which we have considered. Thus theology is eminently practical.

The stories and vignettes collected in this book represent an attempt to display to the church some of its deepest moral convictions in a narrative mode and with a self-consciously theological purpose. 'I have not attempted to speak for the church, but to it.' Besides, the late John W. V. Smith accurately described us when he said that all theological writing in the Church of God movement was (is) one person's voice (1985: 4). No one human being has the right or the authority to tell the church what it ought to be. That is a task that requires the broadest participation of the church. But one person may offer the church a starting point for its deliberation and conversation. In that latter spirit I have written these essays.

The first four chapters display virtues of special importance to the Christian community, the first being hospitality. I have in mind here more than the ability to be a gracious host or hostess. By hospitality I mean that which some have called welcoming the stranger. Hospitality of this sort was a law in many ancient cultures, and the one who failed in his obligation to show hospitality, even to the stranger, was guilty of a serious crime. The second virtue, which is the subject of the reflections in chapter two, is that of fellowship in the body of Christ. The Church of God, for more than a century, has lifted up the idea of the unity of the church. The virtue of fellowship in part expresses our vision of a church beyond division.

The Church of God has written and spoken considerably about truth, and the stories in chapter three consider the virtue of truthfulness. This is a notoriously controversial idea in the last decade of the twentieth century. But truthfulness, beginning with the capacity to see ourselves as we really are, is a virtue indispensable to the people of God. The fourth virtue to be considered is love. This virtue is not the private property of the Church of God movement, and that certainly is not the claim of chapter five. Rather, the stories there explore some of the ways in which we have understood the love that the Holy Spirit pours into the hearts of sincere and faithful Christians.

I am deeply indebted to many people who have contributed in various ways to my thinking. The notes in this book document the work of many people whose ideas I have considered and by which I have been stimulated over the last several years. Some who read this book may be interested in further explorations along lines similar to those mine have taken. To those inquisitive souls I heartily commend the books and articles that are identified in the notes and works cited list at the end.

Nearly all of the material that appears in these pages has been the subject of classroom lectures and discussions at the School of Theology at Anderson University. The students who have populated my courses have helped me more than they realized, and I am grateful for their presence, questions, and arguments. I must also thank many in the church for invitations to hold conferences or lecture about the Church of God and its heritage. Those opportunities to do historical-theological work in the church are extremely important to someone for whom a university campus is the primary location of service.

Placing one's ideas in the hands of colleagues for their criticism and comment is a necessary part of a professor's life. I am grateful to Arthur Kelly and Cole Dawson of Warner Pacific College who read early drafts of some of the essays printed here. My colleagues at the School of Theology and the Bible and Religion Department of Anderson University gave me some of their time in their monthly forum as well as around the tables of the seminary faculty lounge. Their gifts have enriched my life and materially contributed to this book in many, many ways. I must also thank the people who transform my often illegible handwriting into material that others can read. Joyce Krepshaw, faculty secretary at the School of Theology and her student typists, Cheri Waldron and Gina Meyer, lighten my burden immeasurably through their careful, swift, accurate work. Others who write should be as fortunate as I.

Gratitude of a different sort must be expressed to my family. Fran, Ike, and Pete make home a delightful word in my ears—even in the midst of everyday activities like school work, household chores, after-hours band practice, baseball games, and learning to drive. They have been very patient with me and the crabbiness that unfortunately sometimes accompanies my writing projects. Finally, the dedication of this book expresses the gratitude of a son for his parents, who saw to it that his name was inscribed on the Cradle Roll of the nursery of the Church of God at St. Paul Park, Minnesota, an act which introduced him to the narratives of the people of God and their Lord.

Anderson, Indiana
Pentecost 1991

I

The Virtues of the People of God

Hospitality

LESSON IN FRIENDSHIP

Friendship, says Jurgen Moltmann, joins affection and respect. A friend does not expect his or her friend to bow; they look each other in the eye. Friendship, he goes on to say, combines affection and loyalty. You can rely on your friend (115).

John A. D. Khan and George Pease Tasker enjoyed this kind of friendship. Their mutual love of God and passion for the Indian mission field made them colaborers there for more than a dozen years. But "colaborer" only partially describes their relationship.

Perhaps the fact that they were both orphans drew Khan and Tasker together. Alla-ud-Din Khan was born to Muslim parents in East Bengal, India in 1878. At Mymensingh the earnest young man came into contact with some Australian Baptists. Through their teaching from the Sermon on the Mount, Khan's attention was drawn to the words and person of Jesus, and he converted to Christianity in December of 1893.

Khan's family attempted to reclaim him for Islam. For a month they appealed to his love for them. They used magical charms and even hired a Muslim controversialist to argue him back into their faith. When all failed they cast the young man out of their family.

Six years before Khan's birth, George Pease was born in Winnemucca, Nevada. Orphaned early in life, the boy was raised by his aunt in Montreal. He added her name to his and became George Tasker. Possessed of a brilliant mind, George's thirst for learning was unslakeable. He surrounded himself with books and eventually attended McGill University.

George's stepparents intended him for a secular career, and with all his promise he surely would have been successful in business or one of the professions. But against their wishes he associated more and more with a little gathering of the Church of God movement. If he did not actually sever his family ties, Tasker strained them when he announced his intention to follow God's call into the Christian ministry.

Khan, Tasker, and the Church of God came together just as the movement became aware of its foreign mission. Through Khan, India became the second field of Church of God missionary activity. After surveying material from several Christian groups, Khan requested publications of the Gospel Trumpet Company.

That request opened a flow of literature, equipment, and also cash for the relief of victims of the Great Famine of the 1890s. In 1898 Khan opened a missionary home in Calcutta; an orphanage and Bible institute followed. No missionaries had as yet arrived, but the work in India flowered under the leadership of Khan, R. N. Mundul, Mosir Moses, and J. J. M. Roy (later, after he married missionary Evalyn Nichols, he became Nichols-Roy).

This growing Indian church requested the American church to send missionaries to assist them in their great work of spreading the Good News to India's millions. George and Minnie Tasker were among the first generation of missionaries who responded to the Indians' request. George was keenly interested in missions. He had toured India with Hiram Brooks in 1907. A few years later, Tasker sat as a member of the first Missionary Board, serving as secretary-treasurer for its first two years of operations. Then, in 1912 he and his wife accepted India's call.

Tasker did not fit the traditional missionary pattern. Although he worked primarily among educated Indian students and therefore could use English, George learned Urdu

A. D. Khan

A. D. Khan (1878-1922) became aware of the Church of God movement shortly before the turn of the century, and was instrumental in creating the first real missionary awareness in the movement. He toured Church of God congregations in the United States, firing the imaginations of men and women for the infant missionary work. In his native India he led a group of Indian converts in the early days of Church of God work. "The Shelter," a home for Indian girls in Cuttack, is a lasting memorial to Khan's leadership and dedication.

3

George P. Tasker

George P. Tasker (1872-1958) and his first wife, Minnie, were among the first wave of Church of God foreign missionaries. Tasker formed deep friendships with A. D. Khan and D. Otis Teasley. Together they developed a ministerial correspondence course curriculum which was available from the Bible institute sponsored by the New York Missionary Home. Moderates in their theological views, all three men were troubled by what they regarded as a growing sectarianism in the Church of God during the early 1920s.

and Hindi and could understand Bengali. In those days, most missionaries insisted on speaking English and working through translators or requiring English. Such a practice was a not so subtle form of cultural imperialism that fitted well with the colonialism of the early twentieth century. In this view English and American missionaries were the carriers of Christianity and culture. What could the "natives" teach them? George Tasker did not suffer from this disease.

"It was Brother Khan who influenced him greatly as a missionary and enlarged his vision of spiritual things" (Tasker). Few white missionaries were willing to learn much of anything from those to whom they had been sent. Tasker clearly was cut from different cloth. Once, when Khan was so ill that his feet grew painfully cold, Tasker crawled into his friend's sickbed and warmed them with his own body heat.

Khan and Tasker's mutual brilliance, their enthusiasm for the task, and their fellowship in Christ enabled them to look each other in the eye and rely on one another. But Khan died in 1922 of pneumonia when only forty-four years old. Tasker said that his friend didn't struggle against the illness; he just gave up. The Indian church's relationship with the American Missionary Board had not gone well. Khan and Tasker, whose kindred spirits preferred a Christ-centered fellowship to one that was church-centered, did not prosper in a climate that they believed was increasingly sectarian and centrally organized. The Board, on the other hand, was determined to check the independence of the work in India. Certainly in Tasker's mind the deteriorating relationship sapped some of the vitality from his friend's life.

Within two years of Khan's death, five Church of God missionaries in India resigned, George Tasker among them. But India had gotten into his blood and he could not return to North America. He remained there in missionary service until 1946, when he retired to Canada. In 1923 Floyd Heinly was named field secretary for India and thereafter it became a "mission-field" dependent on the Missionary Board. The subsequent history of that relationship has been noteworthy.

5

But how might it have been different had it been guided by the friendship of A. D. Khan and George Tasker?

HAUNTED BY THE PAST

Bill and Gloria Gaither have helped us think of ourselves as a family—the "family of God." If the church is a family, then the church archives might qualify as its hall closet. All sorts of items might be found in there, including some skeletons. A great difference between an archives and the family closet, however, is that the former possesses some built-in controls on when skeletons may be released; the skeletons residing in family closets often escape unpredictably.

We are at a time in the life of the Church of God movement when one of our family skeletons must be unpacked. I am indebted to one of my seminary students, Gregg Giles, for the research that enables me to tell part of the sad story that follows. I write about it in the hope that knowing this story will enable us to live better than some of our forefathers and foremothers in the movement.

At the 1897 Alabama State Camp Meeting, Lena Shoffner rose to preach the sermon of the hour. She looked out on a congregation of people divided by a rope—black people on one side, white people on the other. Her text, in part, was Ephesians 2:14: "For he . . . hath broken down the middle wall of partition between us."

Someone in the crowd could not bear the contradiction between those words and the taut rope dividing Christians in that tent. The rope fell slack, and blacks and whites mingled around an altar of prayer.

Almost immediately some local citizens heard what had happened, and that night a mob went to the campground. Rocks were thrown; buildings were dynamited. Most of the preachers fled into the night.

So much we know from C. E. Brown's *When the Trumpet Sounded*. A wonderful story like that deserves to be remem-

6

bered and retold. But it is here that the skeleton must be let loose.

In 1907 a *Gospel Trumpet* reader wrote to the editor, asking why the paper requested people sending in camp meeting notices to include the word colored if the camp meeting was for blacks. Another person questioned whether members of the two races should greet one another with a holy kiss.

As a matter of fact, during the years after 1897 a variety of questions had been raised in the paper revolving around the question of the degree to which blacks and whites ought to be integrated in the church. The questions all asked essentially the same subject: Just how far does being "one in Jesus" extend?

With growing frequency the *Gospel Trumpet* answered that question in ways that suggest that it listened more to social custom and sentiment than to the Apostle Paul. In 1909 C. W. Naylor wrote that race made no difference in salvation, but he also said that "there are social differences which we cannot ignore without serious consequences. These social differences in no way affect the spiritual unity or fellowship. Both white and colored are better off as a result of social separation than they would be mixed together in these relations" (March 11, page 10).

Within a year the paper took a position that racial separation was preferable to a racially mixed congregation that inhibited evangelistic work among white people. In 1912 blacks were encouraged to hold their own camp meeting so the work could go forth among both peoples. In 1917 at West Middlesex, Pennsylvania, blacks launched their own camp meeting.

So one of our family skeletons is out of the hall closet where all of us can see it and admit that it exists. I doubt that any Christian group would be proud of such a tale. What makes matters worse for us is that this story is part of the larger narrative of a movement of God's people pursuing and testifying to Christian unity. The skeleton not only exists; it haunts us.

Some church growth experts enthusiastically promote what they call the "homogeneous unit principle." Perhaps oversimplified, it means that congregations "grow" best when their members are drawn from largely the same socio-economic class. The early decision of the Church of God to segregate the races where integration hindered evangelism was a seat-of-the-pants version of the homogeneous unit principle. It was wrong in 1910 and remains so today.

May we not ask, with considerable justification, whether we will be the church according to the "homogeneous unit principle" or according to theology? Further, if we say that we will be the church according to theology, must we not hold to Paul's ringing words in Galatians 3:28 regardless of what some people tell us is the best way to "grow a church"?

Because we have believed that in Christ there is neither Jew nor Greek, bond nor free, male nor female, we must confess that this whole sad story is a skeleton in our family closet. But because we still believe these words and we know of the possibility of the new life in Christ to which they testify, we can live with one another in such ways that our children and grandchildren will not be ashamed to tell our stories.

RECEIVING THE CHURCH'S ATTENTION

J. W. Phelps, minister and missions advocate until his death in 1947, carried a particular concern for home missions. You must recall that in the early decades of the twentieth century, Church of God home missions meant urban mission work. Phelps knew that city missions demanded a great deal of their workers. He believed that urban life bred in city residents a "distrust of everyone and everything new." Missions also were forced to compete with "larger numbers of attractions" for the attention of city-dwellers. The religious pluralism of cities further complicated the task of mission workers; the welter of voices made their message more difficult to be heard.

Phelps found particularly disturbing the fact that "the

8

inmates of jails, slums, houses of vice and the street waifs who hardly know right from wrong . . . have received but little special attention from the church." One little missionary home could hardly dare hope to significantly "render spiritual and physical help" to millions of New Yorkers. Still, teeming cities challenged the church's faith and compassion, and Phelps exhorted *Trumpet* readers to "awake to the needs of the hour" (1912:5-6).

The Church of God movement attempted to speak to the needs of the city through the means of missionary homes. Like the majority of American Protestants, early Church of God people markedly preferred rural and small-town life. For the large urban centers of America they reserved names like "Sodom." It seems that our foremothers and forefathers saw only the evil side of urban life.

While they may not have regarded cities positively, the movement's people did not ignore them or give them up to sin and degradation. We have already seen J. W. Phelps' appeal for gospel workers to come to the cities. Thomas and Lillawah Carter wrote to the *Trumpet* in March of 1896, informing readers of their prayers for the establishment of a mission in the "wicked city" of St. Louis. Cities spawned wickedness, but that meant there were souls living there who needed to be rescued.

The Carters made known their prayers for a mission at about the time that missionary homes began popping up in major American cities. Not all the homes were in urban centers. Those that were so situated adapted themselves to care for the special needs of city dwellers, particularly the homeless, jobless, and hungry.

The Open Door Mission occupied the property at 396 Dearborn Street in Chicago. Gorham Tufts, the home manager, reported that the mission fed and housed over ten-thousand people between January 1 and March 10, 1896. Jobless and homeless men seem to have been the mission's primary target. In addition to hearing the gospel preached, those who stayed at Open Door Mission enjoyed the services of a barber, a tailor, and a shoemaker. The home provided these services so the men would appear presentable when they went looking for jobs. Everyone who received assistance from the Chicago mission took a turn working in its wood yard; that was one way the mission defrayed expenses. Even at that it had difficulty paying its way. *Trumpet* editors appendixed a note to Tufts' 1896 article describing the mission's work. They encouraged readers to "put in [their] prayers before the Lord" the fact that the mission lacked a few hundred dollars in rent (Tufts 1896:3).

The Chicago mission's vision and activity changed over the years. A name change signifies its new purpose; the Open Door Mission became the "Faith Missionary Home." In 1910 home manager E. A. Reardon described the home in the *Missionary Herald* (16). He called it "an institution conducted in the interests of the kingdom of God," with the "special object to provide training to missionaries consecrated to the rescuing of souls in this large city." Notice the shift in emphasis. Tufts' report emphasized a ministry to those we have come to refer to as the marginalized. Reardon's report spoke of training. In the shift from direct assistance to training, concern for the marginalized seems to have taken a step away from the center of mission activity.

Training gospel workers was an important feature of nearly all forty-five or so missionary homes that existed during the period from 1890-1925. That may explain one reason why they disappeared. Anderson Bible Training School's emergence as a training center eliminated one of the missionary homes' most important functions. Several of the missionary homes then made a transition into life as settled congregations. What might have happened had the urban missionary homes shifted their emphasis from training back to direct assistance of the marginalized? Perhaps we would have learned better to think of the city as especially needy of the church's attention, just as J. W. Phelps said.

BIG AND BROAD

The news media recently have carried stories about the "Sanctuary Movement." Sanctuary is being offered to re-

Chicago Missionary Home

This building housed the Chicago Missionary Home and Chapel during the early twentieth century. Managers of this home included Gorham Tufts and E. A. Reardon.

The Chicago home undertook rescue mission work as well as training young ministers in gospel work.

11

fugees fleeing violence in some of the countries of Central America. I will not comment on the politics of this controversial situation. But I do wish to use this action by some contemporary American church people as a jumping off point for a discussion of another time, when Church of God people were part of a different sanctuary movement.

The unprecedented destruction of World War II left tens of thousands of Europeans homeless. At the war's end, many others found themselves hundreds of miles from their homes. For still others, home and family had disappeared altogether. All of these were "Displaced Persons,"—DP's in post-World War II jargon.

The Displaced Persons Act of 1950 provided for the relocation of some of these homeless Europeans. In response to this act, the General Ministerial Assembly of the Church of God authorized a Displaced Persons Commission. E. E. Perry chaired the commission, comprised of some fifteen persons. Russell Olt, Dean of Anderson College, chaired its executive committee. The Assembly charged this commission with a two-year assignment to assist in the relocation of as many European Church of God families as possible. At first the commission decided to bring one hundred families over; later they revised their goal upward by doubling it.

In order to relocate in the United States, displaced persons who met all other requirements had to be sponsored by an American family. The commission acted as the facilitator in the lengthy and sometimes tedious process of identifying and qualifying those who might sponsor a homeless family. In some cases American families had acquaintances, friends, or relatives in European Church of God congregations. The commission's first efforts were to arrange for the sponsorship of these as they qualified under the regulations of the Act.

The Church of God commission was too small and its financial resources too limited to allow for its operation independent of other church groups that also had joined the great humanitarian effort. Consequently our commissioners cooperated with Church World Service, an agency of the National Council of Churches. This agency handled all the administrative and clerical work involved in the relocation process. I am intrigued by the obvious absence of any embarrassment about this relationship. The commissioners knew they had not joined the National Council, and they candidly stated their cooperative arrangement; their just and Christian work required it. Indeed, in his final report, Chairman Perry acknowledged the commission's debt to Church World Service.

The commission secured more sponsors than it could place families. Over two hundred sponsors volunteered. By June, 1952, sixty families, more than two hundred people, were relocated in the United States. Another seventy families or parts thereof were rejected for one reason or another. Because the commission had more sponsors than families, they decided to invite Church of God people to sponsor non-Church of God displaced persons. Olt put the matter like this in a letter to each sponsor for whom no family had been identified: "Our commission felt that our church was big enough and broad enough in its sympathies to take at least twenty-five of these non-Church of God families. From a missionary point of view it is a real challenge to our faith . . . We are on the spot, so to speak, as a church in showing our broad sympathy and humanitarianism by so doing."

Broad sympathy, loving concern for the neighbor, a heart large enough to include the stranger and homeless.

SHEEP IN OTHER FOLDS?

In August, 1925 C. J. Blewitt, of the New York City Missionary Home, and Church of God missionary Carl Forsberg attended the Stockholm meetings of the Universal Christian Conference on Life and Work. "Life and Work" was one of the progenitors of the World Council of Churches. Blewitt clearly was impressed by "so many great men and women showing such humility and earnestly seeking to get the world to understand the meaning of love in domestic and public relations" (1925:4-5). Did Blewitt endorse all the aims of "Life and Work?" Of course not. No conference possessed the capacity to replace humanly devised forms, creeds, or ceremonies with the words of Jesus and the apostles. Only the Holy Spirit could truly unify Christians.

In 1927 the other great parent of world ecumenism, the World Conference on Faith and Order, met in Lausanne, Switzerland. R. L. Berry, then F. G. Smith's associate editor at the *Gospel Trumpet*, commented on these meetings. Berry did not expect the conference to advance the cause of Christian unity because it conceived of unity as a world federation of Christians. The Spirit, not federations, united Christians. Berry said he thought the devil would be at the meetings. He followed that judgment however, by saying, "But God will also be there if any of his people are, and we cannot doubt that. So we believe God will be there to inspire his people to real unity such as the Bible demands and inspires" (1927).

Blewitt's and Berry's responses alike illustrate what I have learned to call the virtue of "welcoming the stranger." This virtue has at times prominently displayed itself in the movement's character. In both cases these men embraced the spirit of the ecumenical conferences. As Church of God ministers, they welcomed those who had varying points of view. Neither Blewitt nor Berry doubted that the Spirit of God was present at those meetings. The Spirit's presence ought to form in us the disposition to welcome strangers.

On the other hand, both men clearly saw "Life and Work" and "Faith and Order" to be full of *strangers*. Their hymns, customs, and church traditions all were quite alien to these two Church of God preachers. How could such strangers be embraced? Perhaps Berry and Blewitt understood that all welcomes are not the same. The otherness of the stranger means that his or her welcome will not be charged with the spontaneous warmth of one family member for another. But strangers still may be accorded their own warm welcome.

C. J. Blewitt and R. L. Berry both practiced the virtue of "welcoming strangers." They listened with care and discrimination. They neither accepted nor rejected everything they

New York Missionary Home

The missionary home in New York City, located at 2132 Grand Avenue, served numerous assignments over its lifetime. Like other missionary homes, it served as a training center for young ministers. Evangelists and gospel workers used the home as a base of operations. It served as a kind of hotel for other ministers traveling through New York. The last capacity was especially important since nearly all Church of God missionaries bound for Europe, the Middle East or Africa departed from New York. The missionary home housed many missionaries in transit to their overseas assignments.

R. L. Berry

    R. L. Berry (1874-1952) became F. G. Smith's associate editor at the Gospel Trumpet Company. Berry possessed very strong views on a variety of subjects. This attitude suited him for the role of controversialist. But Berry also could change his mind when persuaded of another position's legitimacy. During the decade of the '20s, for example, Berry completely reversed his position on tithing. An opponent of the "tithe system" at the decade's beginning, he enthusiastically supported tithing less than ten years later.

heard. They carefully weighed the words of strangers, always listening for the Spirit's voice within and hovering beyond the speeches of conferees. Is not such discerning, expectant listening and speaking borne of the awareness that the Holy Spirit blows where it wills—and not only where we desire?

SEEING THE CHURCH

On the corner of Fifth and Chestnut in Anderson a white frame house once stood. For more than thirty-five years the Braille department of the Gospel Trumpet Company occupied this building. Roses grew on the lot, cuttings taken from a Kansas farm where one of the workers, Grace DeFore, was born.

Blind from the age of four, DeFore came to Anderson in 1910 to join the Trumpet family. Along with one or two others she had begun publishing the *Gospel Trumpet* in raised type so the blind also might read the message of the Church of God movement. This work began while Miss DeFore still lived in Pomona, California.

Along with DeFore, Mildred Huston and Nellie Waters formed the staff of this special department. It was special indeed; like DeFore, neither Huston nor Waters could see the fruit of her labor. Nevertheless, they produced Braille editions of the Sunday school curriculum as well as the *Gospel Trumpet*. They also operated a lending library of Braille books. The three women asked visitors for the names of blind persons. As DeFore said, "This is one way we get new readers. Thus all of you can have a part in evangelizing the blind people."

Had you entered the little house on Chestnut Street, you would have seen Grace DeFore answering correspondence, Mildred Huston sterotyping copy for the press, and Nellie Waters wrapping and unwrapping lending library books. Sighted persons provided only minimal assistance.

The literature phase of the Blind department continued until DeFore's retirement in 1953. The lending library continued, but the production of Braille literature ceased, to be replaced by "talking books." Dale Oldham recorded a ten-record volume of C. W. Naylor's, *Secret of the Singing Heart*. Company General Manager Steele Smith hoped that this project would be but the first of many. But eventually the "blind work" ended.

Church of God people once described the ability to grasp the idea of a church beyond division as "seeing the church." The phrase referred to the vision of a church that once again had put on Jesus' seamless robe. Sighted persons were not the only ones who could or did see the church. DeFore, Huston and Waters obviously did, and their vision of Christian unity compelled them to include others who might not see the world of color and light, but who could still see the church.

The consumerist culture in which most of us live shows its insidious nature by threatening to invade the church, too. Some say it already has, as borne out by churches that seem to think that their task is to meet every desire of those to whom the church would minister. I do not mean to suggest that the church should not meet human needs, but not all "needs" qualify for the church's attention. Others, more appropriate to the church's ministry, seem to go begging. Would it not be encouraging to know that growing congregations were filling up with the same lame, halt, and blind who once sought Jesus? Instead we seem to attend to the "needs" of people who are quite like us in many respects. With such a strange idea of needs, do we not often close ourselves off from the handicapped, who might help us to see the church as clearly as these three sightless women?

THE REMARKABLE CASE OF STATE HENRY

Through the lengthening shadows of a late October afternoon in 1902, a convicted killer named Statesville Henry walked to the gallows in the West Virginia State Penitentiary. The Henry case had stirred quite a bit of local attention. Nobody before him had ever been sentenced to death by a Wetzel County court. But that little bit of news seemed like nothing compared to the tangle of events that began to unravel after his trial and conviction.

State Henry maintained his innocence up to the very end of his life. He had been convicted only on the basis of circumstantial evidence, some of it damning. John Rich, the victim of the crime and a laborer on a Short Line railroad gang, was murdered and robbed on payday. Henry could not satisfactorily account for the suspiciously similar amount of money he began spending shortly after Rich's death. Investigators found one of State's coats, bloodstains on its sleeve, stuffed inside his mattress.

The case was clouded, however, by events at Uniontown, Pennsylvania. William Allen, under a death sentence there, told one of his guards that he had killed a man down in Wetzel County and that an innocent man would hang for the crime. Allen planned a dramatic, last-statement confession but was executed before he could make it. Then his guard came forward with the hearsay evidence of Allen's admission, and the plot surrounding State Henry thickened. His lawyer and friends filed appeals and affidavits. Twice Henry received a reprieve. Finally, all avenues of hope exhausted, State Henry was hanged on October 24, 1902.

Marshall County, West Virginia, borders Wetzel County on the north. The town of Moundsville is in Marshall County, and State Henry's case dragged through the courts while the Gospel Trumpet Company made its home in Moundsville. The saints of that Trumpet home knew all about Henry's case. They knew Henry. They called him "Brother State" and he called himself their brother.

While State was confined in the Wetzel County jail, a brother and a sister of the movement visited him. They left behind Enoch Byrum's *The Secret of Salvation*. That book, coupled with their visits, led to Henry's conversion. When State became a Christian he confessed his sins, but he did not number among them the murder of John Rich.

The Trumpet family followed the progress of their brother's case. They visited him after he was transferred to the state prison. They became his public advocates. The case

Stateville "State" Henry (?-1902)

particularly moved Noah and Isabel Byrum, both of whom published poems in his behalf. Ten months before his execution, Henry gave a portrait of himself to J. R. Hale, a relative newcomer to the Church of God movement. On the reverse side of the photograph Henry wrote, "To Dear Brother Hale."

Remember, the prosecutors had built a solid case against State Henry. Public opinion ran strongly against him. On the day of his execution one Moundsville paper described State as "the guiltiest man that ever walked up the steps to that scaffold." But the Trumpet family believed his claim of innocence. On the last day of State Henry's life, some of them could be found in his cell, singing and praying with this condemned man.

In the same year that State Henry died, Noah Byrum compiled a book called *Familiar Names and Faces.* Byrum must have intended the book to be used as a kind of introduction to the Church of God for those people who were unfamiliar with the movement. Photographs of all the famous names and places of the Church of God fill more than half its pages. Along with the photos are published introductory articles about D. S. Warner, the early history of the Gospel Trumpet Company, excerpts from the life of Mother Sarah Smith—and the story of State Henry. Consider this small piece of our history: in a publication designed to put our best foot forward, we included the portrait and story of a condemned man. By visiting State in prison, by praying and singing with him on his last day, by including his story and face with all the rest of ours, perhaps we did put our best foot forward back there in 1902.

THE GERMAN TRIANGLE

The Church of God's ethnic diversity in its early years both puzzles and encourages me. The movement came into being at a time when many Americans feared the immigrants streaming into the nation. Yet foreign language work among Greeks, Hungarians, Scandinavians, and others began early

21

enough and in such numbers that the 1917 edition of the *Yearbook* listed each language that a preacher could use. Someone thought that the ability to speak a language other than English augmented a person's ministerial credentials.

The oldest and largest of these foreign language efforts involved the Germans. A sizeable part of the early gospel efforts of Church of God preachers occurred within a region commonly known as the "German Triangle." Imagine the territory between the cities of St. Louis, Cincinnati, and Milwaukee. In and near this area many German immigrants had settled. Thick German accents flavored the English of some of the earliest converts to the Church of God way.

In November 1895, one of these converts reported the evangelistic work being conducted among Germans in Milwaukee and also at Baraboo out in south-central Wisconsin. Fred Hahn and W. P. Halbesleben labored on this stony ground. Not only was Milwaukee "Satan's Seat," but some of Hahn's brothers and sisters in the Lord criticized him for remaining too long in the field and neglecting the people at home.

For nearly a year Hahn had edited and published *Die Evangeliums Posaune*, a German language version of the *Gospel Trumpet*. Eventually some three thousand persons paid for subscriptions to this little paper. Enthusiasm for a German language paper had been growing for two or three years even before the first issue came out. In his report from Milwaukee, Hahn included translations of testimonies written by Ida Meyer and Robert Leudtke. Both of them praised the power of God unto salvation and Ida thanked God for the *Posaune*. It had been the special medium through which God had enriched her life.

The German language work spread throughout North America and beyond because of the commitment and ingenuity of people like Fred Hahn. Eventually more than two dozen German language congregations were founded. From those congregations came pastors, missionaries, and teachers who blessed the lives of others, some of whom could speak German, but most of whom could not.

That such a work began at a time of ethnic and racial suspicion does not make much sense. It was neither prudent nor expedient. The Church of God movement in general and the publishing work in particular possessed only the scantiest of resources. Somebody legitimately could have complained that another new venture would tax those resources beyond their limits.

That such a project could begin in unfavorable circumstances suggests that visions and ideas can prompt people to action. People like Fred Hahn were captivated by a particular idea of the church. That vision extended across time and space, across all the other barriers we humans either construct or allow to divide us. At times it is easy to believe that Hahn and all the others were right to be captive to such an idea.

WELCOMING THE STRANGER

For several obvious reasons, war is a frightening human invention. Its business is destruction—of material, of will, of life. William Tecumseh Sherman, who marched Union soldiers from Atlanta to the sea during the last months of the American Civil War, summarized the matter well when he said simply, "War is hell."

Like those that came before and after, World War I was a devastating war, not only in Europe, but in the United States as well. Most of the war's destruction was visited on soldiers and civilians in Europe. But in the United States, another of war's frightening aspects reared its ugly head. This particular dimension touched the lives of many who were still newcomers to American life.

At the turn of the century, the United States' population included millions of people who were foreign born. Slightly more than eight-million Europeans entered the United States during the period from 1901-1910 alone, but during the "Great War" concern about the loyalty of these millions of new Americans focused particularly on one group, the German immigrants. They were a sizeable minority, nearly four million of them having immigrated between 1871 and 1910. Many feared that German-Americans would be loyal to the Kaiser rather than America.

Fear of these German-American strangers prompted some Americans to attack them. Persons with readily identifiable German surnames suddenly became suspect. Their business was no longer welcome in certain stores. Threats of violence were made against some. Anti-German sentiment caused many of these immigrants to change their names: "Schmidt" became "Smith," and so forth. Thousands of others simply avoided contact with "Americans" whenever possible.

All of this is background to some events that occurred in Anderson, Indiana in 1918. In the autumn of that year officers of the Gospel Trumpet Company were visited by representatives of the Madison County Council of Defense. The Council had organized out of a concern for the presence of Germans and pro-German sentiment in central Indiana. They knew that the Gospel Trumpet Company operated a German department that published an edition of the *Trumpet* in that language for the edification of German immigrants in the United States and for Germans in Germany. Council representatives visited the company one October day to encourage them to cease publication of the German language paper "on account of prevailing sentiment."

How would the board of directors respond to such a request and the threat it only thinly veiled? What could they have deliberated? They might have said, "We need to keep good relations with the community." Or they might have said, "This anti-German attitude borders on hysteria, and we must strike a blow for reason and tolerance." Or they may have said, "The message we seek to communicate to our German-speaking brothers and sisters outweighs the request of the defense council." Their reason may have been one of these latter statements or some other, but in any case on October 3, the board of directors voted to continue German language publications "for the present."

Why is this small incident important? It illustrates a quality in the character of some early Church of God people. Much has been made of the early movement's desire to avoid contact with "the world." But the board of directors' decision illustrates another quality of the early Church of God: at times we have been a people capable of welcoming strangers. German-Americans were "strangers and aliens in the land" in the fall of 1918. Many in America thought of them that way. But the Trumpet board of directors refused to segregate German speaking people. Though strangers, potentially even enemies, they received the movement's welcome.

What is significant about the capacity to welcome strangers? Why is it important for us to be people who possess such a virtue? Our capacity to welcome strangers depends, in large measure, upon our memory that we, too, once were strangers. Once we were far from God, yet God loved us, welcomed us. When we were yet strangers and aliens the church received us to its bosom. We came to God and the church as prodigal children, alienated yet awaited by those who sat at the window watching for us, the welcome already lighting their eyes. Dare we ever forget that once we were strangers needing a welcome? Do we not owe the same welcome to those unlike us who already are outside our door?

Welcoming the stranger is an act based in the memory that we, too, once were strangers. But there is another reason for us to welcome the stranger. The strange, new person or the new idea may carry a word from God addressed to us. The new thought or idea must be tested, of course. But it must also be heard. Moses returned from Midian as a stranger to an oppressed and enslaved Israel; Jesus undertook a wanderer's life-style, making himself everywhere without home and everywhere a stranger, to speak God's word to his people. The truth God has for us may come from new and unexpected quarters. Thus we must continue to be people with the capacity to welcome strangers.

CANDINAVIANS AT ST. PAUL PARK

At the foot of Broadway Street in the village of St. Paul Park, Minnesota, near the eastern bank of the Mississippi River, stands a moderately sized brick, two-story building. It has known several owners and tenants. The current owner, Ashland Petroleum Company, has painted the building all blue, white, and red and emblazoned a large "SuperAmerica" sign on the building's side. Before its life as an oil refinery storehouse, the building housed a brass factory.

Neither of those enterprises is as interesting and helpful to us as the story of some people who moved into that building in 1903. They spent about four-hundred dollars remodeling it in order to publish a religious paper known as the *Den Evangeliske Basun*. In Dano-Norwegian, the mother tongue of these people, the paper's title meant the *Gospel Trumpet*.

The people who leased that brick building at the foot of Broadway called themselves the *Evangeli Basun* Publishing Company. Their special burden was the spread of the message of the Church of God movement among their Dano-Norwegian and Swedish speaking fellow immigrants. The company had begun in Thomas and Keo Nelson's kitchen in Muscatine, Iowa in 1900. Two years later it moved into the second story of C. G. Neils' Grand Forks (North Dakota) Steam Laundry. From 1903 until 1923 the company was located in St. Paul Park. In the latter year the publication of the papers was transferred to Sweden and Denmark. A bi-monthly version of *Den Evangeliske Basun* continues to be published in Denmark to this day.

Camp meetings were great times of spiritual refreshment and fellowship for these Scandinavian immigrants, even as they were for the saints who gathered at Moundsville, West Virginia and later Anderson or any one of several dozen other sites. But one characteristic that made camp meetings at St. Paul Park, Grand Forks, or Arlington, South Dakota a little different from their American counterparts was the fact that the former always included full preaching services in at least two and often three or more languages.

Had you attended Grand Forks Camp Meeting in 1903 you might have heard preaching in German, Norwegian, Swedish, or English. Readers of *Den Evangeliske Basun* were encouraged not to be intimidated by language differences and come to camp meeting anyway. The widely traveled Norwegian-American preacher Sven O. Susag testified to the miraculous ability of his American listeners to understand his Norwegian sermons, and an itinerant bookseller named Olai Christoffersen wrote that the Lord had blessed him at English language meetings even when he had not understood much of the preaching.

Language differences pose a formidable barrier to Christian fellowship and understanding. But part of the witness of people like Nelson, Susag, and Christoffersen is their stubborn refusal to allow the construction of language barriers. They wanted to be understood; they also wanted to understand.

The early Scandinavians in the Church of God overcame barriers to fellowship for reasons other than their simple desire to be understood. The most important of them is found in lyrics that C. T. Langeson wrote for a song often used by the Scandinavian immigrants in their communion services. Its title was "Remember Jesus." The words of one verse say

> One bread, one body we,
> His church and bride so dear

United in mind and spirit
With love's almighty bond.

A united fellowship was possible because of the presence of love. This love was more than a "warm fuzzy." It was a life-style of servanthood "which Jesus would have in his church here on earth." This love was the work of the sanctifying Spirit. A united church was possible in the presence of the kind of love in which human beings serve each other in the name of Jesus. Such love destroys all manner of barriers, whether language or any other we erect when we refuse to be understood—or to understand.

A LITTLE BAND OF US

The American presidential campaign of 1884 set new levels of lowness. Republican clergy, desperately seeking the election of their man, James G. Blaine, labeled the Democrats and Grover Cleveland as the party of "Rum, Romanism, and Rebellion." Democrats attacked Blaine as a candidate tattooed with numberless political dishonesties. Republicans were delighted to learn that Cleveland had fathered an illegitimate son. Small wonder that you can read articles in the *Gospel Trumpet* of that year that lament the nation's sorry condition.

In May of 1884 Edna Finch and Emily Barnes wrote letters to the *Trumpet* office, recently relocated in more spacious quarters in Williamston, Michigan. Both their letters reflected the fact that Thomas G. Warren had started a prayer meeting at Geneva Center, Michigan. Emily attended those meetings and was converted in one of them. She invited Edna to attend and shared with her friend some copies of the *Trumpet*. Edna, too, experienced regeneration and sanctification in Brother Warren's meetings. Of the group Emily wrote: "There is a little band of us here, but glory to God, we have glorious meetings, and the Lord adds to the church daily those being saved" (1884).

D. S. Warner formed the first "evangelistic company"

during the Williamston years. Along with him, Sarah Smith, Nannie Kigar, Frances (Frankie) Miller, and Barney Warren modeled a style of evangelism that others followed. These were the "flying messengers." They *evangelized* more than they "planted churches." They saw a need to broadcast their message as widely as possible. Establishing churches was not their primary goal.

In those early days of the movement, "meetings" served as focal points—camp *meetings*, assembly *meetings*, grove *meetings*, brush arbor *meetings*. The term connotes more of a sense of activity than the static nouns *church* or *congregation*. A meeting requires coming and going; it is temporary. Camp meetings of today resemble reunions, for there we often see old friends from the past. But the early meetings of the movement offered occasions to get acquainted, often for the first time. The August 1, 1884 issue of the *Trumpet* announced a grove meeting in Medina County, Ohio. Ezra Smith, said the paper, would meet railroad travelers at the Burbank station—if they sent advance notice of their arrival times. Along with Warner, Joseph and Allie Fisher planned to attend and concluded their announcement by saying, "*We would love to meet* many of the dear followers of the Lamb at that meeting" (Warner 1884, emphasis added).

In the movement's early years, the saints prized the simple event of meeting together as the church rather than "establishing" it. That is understandable, for the early saints of the movement often isolated themselves as they shook the denominational dust from their feet. Rachel Burton, writing from Albion, Indiana, closed her letter, "Your sister, standing alone with Jesus" (1884). Warner often titled his appeals for financial support "To the Saints *Abroad*." In those early years the saints resembled the Jews of the Diaspora.

More than anything else, the *Gospel Trumpet* itself held the movement together in its first decades. It announced meetings and locations. It published testimonies. It reported successful Bible-study meetings like the one begun by Thomas Warren. Others read those reports and followed his example and that of countless others.

Tabernacle at Anderson

Pictured here is the congregation gathered in the old tabernacle at Anderson Camp Meeting in 1950. The occasion was the World Service Day Worship.

31

An important point to remember is that these were *meetings*—gatherings for prayer and the earnest study of the Scriptures. Although they did not say it precisely in such words, their practice of church strongly suggests that they thought of "church" as a verb—motion and activity. That is a conception of the church worth pondering as we consider "planting" churches.

ONE HEART AND SOUL AND MIND

Language has the power to shape our perceptions and thus the reality in which we live. According to some who work in this area a great deal more than I, the language we use to describe ideas or experiences is not passive. Instead, it actually shapes our ideas or experiences. Let me explain by referring to two very different and deeply loved gospel songs out of the movement's past.

In 1895, only months before his death, Daniel S. Warner wrote "The Bond of Perfectness." As best I can determine, this song first appeared in *Select Hymns* (1911). In eloquent simplicity it conveys Warner's mature ideas about Christian unity: "How this perfect love unites us all in Jesus."

Perfect love was a synonym for the experience of entire sanctification. It came through the activity of the Holy Spirit. Interpreting the song he wrote, Warner's message about the oneness of God's people might be summarized as follows: Unity comes in the sanctifying presence of the Holy Spirit. Certainly God the Holy Spirit authors the unity of the church. Thus Warner wrote in the chorus: "One heart and soul and mind we prove the union *heaven gave* us" (emphasis added). We do not achieve unity; we do not manufacture it. It is the product of the sanctifying activity of the Holy Spirit.

I wonder what Warner had in mind by the phrase "one *heart* and *soul* and *mind*." Union of hearts and souls I can rather readily understand. But oneness of mind? Did Warner think that sanctification would result in everyone thinking alike? I think not. But can we not have singleness of mind in the sense that Paul used in Philippians 2, "Have the same commitments, the same single-minded vision as Christ?" (my paraphrase) We know of the Spirit's *harmonizing* of minds while they continued to think differently. Is that not being of one mind?

A few years after the appearance of "The Bond of Perfectness," C. W. Naylor published "The Church's Jubilee" in *Reformation Glory* (1923). Now we had a real marching song to express the growing conviction that unity lay in uniform beliefs. "Jubilee" carries on the tradition of W. G. Schell's older, but far less singable, "Biblical Trace of the Church." In both cases, however, the emphasis on unity is subtly shifted away from the point made in "The Bond of Perfectness." In "Jubilee" the church's unity also rests in its having one mind, but now understood as a common way of reading certain books of the Bible. Unity here becomes the result of common *beliefs*. The tacit assumption is that we are united as long as we share the same beliefs. But if that is true, then one would have to say that Peter and Paul were not united when Paul, in his words, "withstood Cephas to his face."

On the contrary, I think Peter and Paul were in unity even as they stood eyeball to eyeball. Their dispute occurred in the presence of the sanctifying Spirit. Despite deep differences of opinion about important matters, Peter and Paul continued to trust one another. Neither of them questioned their common *experience* of heart and soul in Christ. Obviously they did not think alike, but both sought the mind of Christ. Only the sanctifying Spirit can work such unity in the face of the multiplied differences that are part of what it means to be a human living in the time and space of this world. Maybe D. S. Warner saw that in the union that heaven gave us.

Return now to the theme that opened our conversation. If language does indeed have the power to shape the reality in which we live, then it also will have shaped our experience of the Church of God movement. Some of us have experienced the movement, and our lives have been accordingly

33

shaped, in language that derives from the ideas and spirit of the "Bond of Perfectness." Others of us have an experience that derives the spirit and themes of "The Church's Jubilee." These two ways of being differ in major ways. Such differences require of us the most honest, searching inquiry and conversation about the nature of Christian unity. But these differences entitle none of us to a reality smaller than the circle of God's love.

GOD'S WAYS ARE NOT OUR WAYS

Suppose you go to church next Sunday morning as usual. An usher will greet you with a familiar handshake and smile, then show you to your pew. Would you be surprised if the usher did not hand you a "bulletin?" (How the order of service came to have this name I do not know. The usage we have given the word as equivalent to "worship folder" does not fit standard dictionary definitions). How would you know what numbers to sing and when to pray? When to give your offering? When to get ready for the sermon?

Once upon a time in the Church of God, "bulletins" did not exist. No one would have dared to use one, for they were condemned as but one more form of the "man-rule" (whether male or female) we regarded as part of sect-Babylon. Something like a preplanned worship order gave evidence that its preparer must be usurping the work of the Holy Spirit. The Spirit leads to all truth (John 16:13), therefore the church should allow the Spirit to lead, and the way to do that was to shun man-rule, whether in worship or in the organization of the church.

Early in the history of the movement we favored what was called "charismatic leadership." The Spirit led the church by inspiring and gifting the members for various leadership roles, hence the term charismatic, from *charismata*, i.e., spiritual gifts. It is a shame that charismatic has been so strongly linked to one particular phenomenon that we are reluctant to use this word that makes such an important point in our understanding of the church.

34

If the Holy Spirit is the leader, the guide, the animating force of the church, then we have hit on the same idea that Paul expressed by calling the church the body of Christ. We who claim the Spirit's leadership thus have what could be called an incarnational model of the church. We, the church, become the corporate, present form of the incarnation, continuing Jesus' work in the world today. All this because we say the Holy Spirit guides us into the truth.

We did not stay with the no-organization policy for very long. Within twenty-five years of Warner's death we created the General Ministerial Assembly. Warner so believed in charismatic leadership that he opposed the practices of formal assemblies and, especially, voting. But in the new Assembly votes were counted to determine the membership of committees, boards, and the like. It may not have been all bad, the idea of voting. C. E. Brown, fourth editor of the *Gospel Trumpet*, said that in "spiritual democracies" the Spirit could inspire people to vote for the divinely appointed person. His idea of "spiritual democracy" caught the movement's fancy precisely at a time when democracy was an idea for which many were fighting and dying—the 1930s and 1940s.

The idea of democratically grounded leadership recently was extended by the General Assembly. Ballot-by-mail will be in limited use because of action taken by the 1987 Assembly. It seems a good thing to do, giving as many people as possible the opportunity to vote on matters that affect the life of the movement. It certainly is the *democratic* thing to do.

In advocating "charismatic leadership" the Church of God put forth the idea that the church was uniquely governed, that typical political forms were not adaptable to the church. Democracy, oligarchy, monarchy—nothing from political culture fit the idea that the church was divinely ordered. What an astounding claim! How impractical! How problematic! Still, if the church is more than a collection of individuals, if it is a way of witnessing to the world of a new way of living together made possible by Christ, then perhaps we should not be so hasty to borrow from the prevailing political culture.

Surely we do not need to be reminded that God's ways are not ours. But then the task for us will not be to baptize our ways, but learn God's. Then we, too, can be led by the Spirit.

BLESS GOD FOR THE DEPRESSION

Some thirteen million Americans looked for work in 1932. The Great Depression sent good, hard-working people out on the street—or on the road—looking for any kind of work. For some the only work to be found was selling apples on street corners. Those fortunate enough to keep their jobs often saw their wages cut and cut again. During a three-year span of depression years, the Gospel Trumpet Company reduced its payroll by fifty percent. Some came by way of salary and wage cuts, some by way of lay-offs.

In the depression years of 1932-33, Axchie Bolitho completed her sixth year as pastor of the Church of God at 2132 Grand Avenue in the Bronx, New York. Formerly this congregation was known as the New York Missionary Home. Twenty-five years earlier, D. O. Teasley had superintended the home and construction of the building used by the congregation there down through the years.

Today we would call the New York church "missions minded." Church of God missionaries *enroute* to assignments in Europe, Africa, or the Middle East found a warm welcome and accommodations at the New York home. The congregation itself sent many of its own into missionary service. Ten men and women, some with children, left the New York congregation as missionaries in the years from 1907-1933. Workers from the home began mission congregations in Harlem and other neighborhoods of the city.

What was important to the women and men of the New York church during the throes of the Great Depression? We might answer such a question by looking at their budget. On October 1, 1932, they had a bank balance of $191.99. Total

Axchie F. Bolitho

Axchie F. Bolitho (1886-1974) was one of the many gifted women who were called to ordained ministry in the Church of God. Bolitho's gifts and abilities were applied to a variety of ministerial roles: pastor, teacher, curriculum writer, worker at Gospel Trumpet Company editorial assignments. She published a biography of songwriter Barney Warren entitled *To the Chief Singer.*

37

receipts for the year just concluded were $3,663.43. Of that amount more was given to missions and relief than to the pastor, who received $1,300.

Sometimes congregations expressly state their deepest convictions. The New York congregation published a list of ideas for which they stood. One reads, for example, (a) "that indifference to or willfull (*sic*) rebellion against the will and authority of God is sin"; (b) "that the Holy Bible is the Word of God written first in the minds and hearts of those who sought Him and afterwards by them in books for the edification and instruction of all succeeding generations"; (c) "that war is an unmitigated evil for the abolition of which the church must work"; (d) "that race, color and class prejudices are all contrary to the Christian spirit"; (e) "that the profit motive in business must be displaced by the motive of good will."

The congregation stated these convictions and others in their yearbook for 1932-33. They paid for this handsome little booklet by selling advertising space to the neighborhood businesses. Could those businesses have known the kind of economics their contributions supported?

Half the yearbook was taken up with advertisements. Tailors, restaurants, dairies, confectioners, a roller-skating arena, and dozens of others advertised in the New York church yearbook. Even "P. Greenblatt" advertised his shop, which sold stationery, cigars, cigarettes, candies, and ice cream.

For more than half a century the Missionary Home stood as a witness to Christ amid the teeming multitudes of New York. The shape of that ministry changed often through the years—from missionary training center and hostel to settled congregation. The New York home later boarded Church of God graduate students attending Columbia University and Union Theological Seminary. The changing forms of its ministry always expressed its spiritual center. Thus Pastor Bolitho could introduce a meditation on Psalm 73 with this sentence: "If these days of depression shall suffice to restore to us a sense of spiritual values, as his depression did the

Psalmist, then shall we say: 'Bless God for the depression.'"

GOD CALLS THE MINISTERS

In 1884 D. S. Warner formed the first "evangelistic company" of the reformation movement. Along with himself it included Barney Warren, Frankie Miller, Nannie Kigar, and Sarah Smith. Three women and two men, none of them married to each other, was a traveling arrangement certain to spawn Victorian-type rumors in some of the places they visited. Eyebrows must have been raised at the sight of them riding on their wagon, singing their way into town. This company stayed together for a little more than four years, evangelizing the Midwest and southern Canada. "Mother" Smith said that during those years the five of them traveled in perfect harmony. "They were dearer to me than my own relatives" (n.d. 17). That is an extraordinary sentence. But Mother Smith was an extraordinary woman.

Sarah Sauer Smith was born into a Lutheran family in Summit County, Ohio. She was reared, as she put it, a "strictly moral girl," who received very little public education or religious instruction. She experienced conversion in 1842 but was mystified about why Christians felt the need to divide themselves into denominations. Sarah belonged to a local holiness association, and through their common commitment to the doctrine of holiness, Mrs. Smith met D. S. Warner and cast her lot with the Church of God reformation movement.

Mother Smith was sixty-one years old when Warner asked her to join his company. She was married to a farmer who, by the way, had not been invited on this evangelistic mission. Who did Warner consider himself that he would even think of making such a request, and why would Sarah dare consider accepting the invitation?

Imagine Mother Smith telling her son, "Dan, I'm done cooking for farming." Nothing happens for the next few minutes except her weeping. Then Dan says, "Well mother, if you have any other work to do besides cooking, the

Warner Evangelistic Company

Pictured here is the Warner evangelistic company: l-r, Barney Warren, D. S. Warner, Nannie Kigar, "Mother" Sarah Smith and Frankie Miller. The evangelistic company was the backbone of the "flying ministry" in the early days of the Church of God movement. Companies of three, four or five individuals traveled about the countryside, singing and preaching in meetings which they gathered spontaneously. Evangelistic companies were preferred over settled pastorates in the movement's early days.

sooner you get at it the better it will be." Then came the same announcement to her husband.

"How soon will you have to leave?" he asked.

"Ten days or two weeks."

"I'll get you some money."

Mother Smith explained this extraordinary action by saying in eloquent simplicity that "the Lord had a work for me to do different from what I had been doing."

Perhaps Farmer Smith had been reading the *Gospel Trumpet* and espoused its open attitude toward women in ministry. W. G. Shell, in the February 24, 1898 issue, responded to a questioner who wanted to know what Schell believed about married women in gospel work. Schell said that because in Christ there is neither male nor female" God sometimes calls married women into the work as ministers, helpers, etc., in which case they are released from their work as housekeeper just as a man is released from 'working with his hands.' "

Why quote W. G. Schell? Certainly it is not to authorize the disruption of marriages and homes. But this early attitude of the Church of God toward women in ministry is worth remembering, considering, and discussing. Ministry was regarded by our forefathers and foremothers as a life-work validated by divine calling. Just as God alone set members in the church, so God alone called ministers to serve that church. Whether those ministers happened to be men or women was apparently not one of God's considerations. Since God did not fret over ministerial maleness or femaleness, neither should it matter in God's church.

Scarcely more than a month before Mrs. Smith's obituary appeared in the *Gospel Trumpet*, this question appeared in the "Questions Answered" feature of the paper, "Is it legal for a woman to preach the gospel?" The anonymous questioner was corrected by J. W. Byers; what mattered was whether it was *scriptural* for women to preach. Seven New Testament references provided Byers' affirmative reply. Five weeks later the questioner could have read another kind of answer in the obituary's summary of the life of Mother Sarah Smith. One hopes that it was so.

A REASON FOR BEING

When the *Gospel Trumpet* moved from Williamston to Grand Junction in 1886 more changed than the company's mailing address. Williamston lays east of Lansing, Grand Junction west of Kalamazoo. The two villages are not far apart, less than a hundred miles as the crow flies. But a critical change in the movement's self-understanding occurred after the move to Grand Junction.

Not very far from Grand Junction lies Battle Creek, a name now associated with breakfast cereal. Not altogether coincidental is the fact that it also had been a center of Adventist activity and influence. Since the 1840s Adventists of one form or another had concerned themselves with discerning the signs of the end of time. One of their leading authorities on this subject was a man named Uriah Smith, who published his interpretation of the apocalyptic books of the Bible in 1881 in the volume *Thoughts, Critical and Practical, on the Books of Daniel and the Revelation.* In this book Smith laid out a line of historical development that validated the existence of the Adventists by means of biblical prophecy. This gave his group a self-understanding and a reason for being.

The close proximity of Battle Creek to Grand Junction suggests the idea that contacts between Adventists and Church of God people increased after 1886. One may also surmise that an air of debate characterized many of those meetings. Both groups competed for the attention of the same southwest Michiganders. We might say that the Church of God and Adventists competed for the same religious turf in that part of the world.

Skilled debaters become thoroughly familiar with the arguments of their opponents. D. S. Warner did just that. In his library, now housed in the School of Theology Archives, rests a copy of Uriah Smith's book. Certain sections Warner read very carefully for he underlined them, and their margins have notes written in Warner's handwriting. One or two sheets of paper with additional notes also are inserted into the pages of Smith's book.

Thoughts on Daniel and the Revelation impressed D. S. Warner. In fact, the main lines of Smith's argument convinced him of the merit of this system of interpretation. But Warner also believed that certain aspects required modification. For one thing, Daniel and the Revelation must certainly point to some group other than Uriah Smith's Adventists. Warner thus took over Smith's interpretive system (which we call *church-historical*) but modified some of its important details. Warner's death halted his work on a large manuscript in which he interpreted Daniel and Revelation typologically and church-historically. H. M. Riggle edited and completed this work, published as *The Cleansing of the Sanctuary* in 1903. Now the Church of God had a self-understanding to ground its sense of purpose.

In the last decade of the nineteenth century and the first two of the twentieth, this apocalyptically charged self-understanding lent high resolve to many people in the movement. For them the movement's reason for being could be documented in the charts from which lectures were often drawn, showing the Church of God movement to be the time of the evening light prophesied by Zechariah. Such a self-understanding contributed to their self-confidence and enabled them to sing confidently, "There's a mighty reformation sweeping o'er the land."

The apocalyptic self-understanding answered the important question that congregations and church groups must frequently ask themselves: "Why are we here? What is our reason for being?" The apocalyptically minded answer by saying, "Because we are prophesied to be a part of God's grand activity at the end of time."

Some in the Church of God movement remain of the apocalyptic mind-set. They have a self-understanding and reason for being. How might these have been different had the Trumpet Company moved from Williamston to Indianapolis, a center of the restorationist Christian churches movement?

43

Others in the Church of God are less apocalyptically minded—perhaps not at all. But that does not free them of the questions, Who are we?, Why are we here?, and Who is it that God calls us to be?

MINISTERIAL VOCATION

Abraham Isaac Jacob Jackson, a Michigan Baptist farmer-preacher who once had worn the yoke of slavery, believed in prayer. Any time or place suited him for communion with God. Jackson frequently laid before the Lord his desires for the realization of the church of the New Testament and, second, that one of his fifteen children would be called into ministry.

The fourteenth of those children, Raymond, heard his father pray those two concerns, and in Raymond's mind they were related: Abraham hoped that one of his children would catch the vision of Christian unity. Raymond S. Jackson later responded to a divine vocation to ministry.* His long and distinguished years of service as a minister of the Church of God movement eloquently answered his father's prayer. Although he pastored seven different congregations in Indiana, Kansas, Missouri, and Michigan, his name is most commonly associated with works in Detroit.

Raymond Jackson cared about leadership and the training of workers in the church. He and his wife, Cleopatra, distinguished themselves in the field of leadership development. The Board of Christian Education of the Church of God recognized their achievement and publicly wished that others might model themselves after the Jacksons.

Cleopatra and Raymond knew that leaders do not simply spring into being, fully formed and ready to take up positions of responsibility. Leaders must be developed, which is to say, educated. One must not, however, think of education as the mere acquisition of technique. Leadership is more than a matter of simply learning "how to." Leaders develop as their character is formed toward a particular goal. That means that the education of leaders requires the presence of exemplary persons as teacher-models of those whom God calls to leadership. Ministers, by the example of how they live out their own vocation, are crucial to the development of future ministers.

Raymond Jackson afforded many young people the opportunity to observe, at close hand, an exemplary ministry. As he practiced his vocation he created in others the question whether they, too, might serve God and neighbor in such a capacity. Those who responded he personally encouraged. He also created opportunities for young ministers to serve and thus learn some of the arts of ministry. Jackson not only offered the example of his life. He also guided the lives of others. One should not be surprised to discover that Jackson more than once laid his hand on the shoulder of a bright-eyed, inquisitive adolescent and inquired whether God might want that person for ministry.

We can make the ministerial vocation too much captive to the individualized and privatized gospel of our age. We can make "the call" too mystical, too much a matter of people's "personal affairs" and thus convince ourselves that we should never meddle there. Thank God that Abraham Jackson's desire for a child to follow him in the ministry was audible; we may date the beginning of Raymond's vocation from the time his father's words first fell on his ear. I do not mean to suggest that Raymond's ministerial vocation was not from God. But Abraham had something to do with it. In the same manner, Raymond's later practice of ministry surely stimulated the ministerial vocation of others.

The ministry is not a job. Neither is it a career. It can be properly described only as a vocation. In that sense we may never say "*my* ministry." The ministry always is God's, but it is entrusted to us.

How does this calling come to men and women in the church? Is it exclusively a matter of personal insight or inspiration? Fortunately we have Raymond Jackson's example to show us that the ministerial vocation is also public. Abraham prayed in public. Raymond's inspiring example was public. He created opportunities for young leaders to practice ministry and confirm their vocation in public.

At this moment in the life of American culture, when people are excessively preoccupied with private interests and the accomplishment of personal goals, Raymond Jackson's public vocation and ministry offer important correctives to these mistaken notions of modernity. Leadership for the church—lay and ministerial—still needs to be developed, publicly.

AN ALTERNATIVE TO VIOLENCE

In terms of sheer bloodshed, the most violent period in American history extended from 1861 to 1865. Southerners call this the "War Between the States," and Yankees call it the "Civil War." Either name labels the bloodiest war in American history. More Americans were killed in this one war than all the casualties of all the other wars in which American soldiers have fought.

The first generation of leadership in the Church of God movement knew firsthand the horrors of the Civil War. Many of them were young people during the war years. Some of them carried arms. The Archives at the School of Theology possesses photocopies that document a portion of the career of one of those soldiers—private Daniel S. Warner, Company C, 195th Ohio Volunteer Infantry Regiment.

Warner was twenty-two years old when he joined the Union Army. The war lasted scarcely more than a month after he volunteered and collected his one-hundred dollars enlistment bounty. Although he enlisted for a year's tour of duty, by August he had been discharged. During a forced march to Berryville, Virginia, and on toward the Shenandoah Valley, Warner developed a serious lung condition. His poor health led to an honorable discharge from the Army in July 1865. His period of service lasted less than five months. Twenty-five years later he applied for and received a soldier's disability pension that paid him twelve dollars per month.

Early Church of God people were familiar with violence in forms other than the organized violence of war. Some of those people were pelted with rocks, threatened with tar and feathers and dynamited out of buildings in which they worshiped. The film *Heaven to Earth* contains a memorable scene in which a gang of young toughs attempts to break up a prayer meeting of the saints. Violence breaks out and the prayer meeting's leader is hurt. His attacker then sees himself for what he has done and kneels in a prayer of repentance that seeks both the forgiveness of God and the young man's victim.

I do not know whether or not this scene is drawn from an actual historical account, but I do know that Barney E. Warren wrote a gospel song in 1897 entitled "The Kingdom of Peace." That song intertwines the themes of holiness, unity, and peace in a way that might instruct us as we contemplate the Church of God movement in our own violent society.

Consider the proposition that violence and idolatry are directly related; the greater the falsity of the objects we worship, the greater we are tempted to defend them with violence. But one must also consider the possibility that the church is God's alternative to human forms of society, prone as they are to resort to violence. The church extends across the barriers of time, space, and language, which become human pretexts for misunderstanding, hatred and, ultimately, violence. The church witnesses to a unity that does not erase those barriers; it transcends them. The church, which witnesses to the peace of God's reign by word and deed, is God's earthly alternative to worldly violence. So those in whom God's unity is worked by the power of the sanctifying Spirit—the church—stand as God's judgment against this world and its all-too-frequent use of violence to gain its false ends. Did Barney Warren have such ideas in mind when he wrote his song about God's peace in our hearts? I hope so. I hope we do when we sing it.

A HELPFUL HISTORY

Together we go to tell our neighbors
The message of Christ, our truest Friend.
All power is His, pow'r in earth and heaven,
And He will be with us to the end.

Frederick Shackleton wrote those words to help launch a great campaign in the Church of God movement. The title of this campaign was the "Mid-Century Evangelistic Advance." As the title suggests, the campaign focused the movement's attention on the future and the possibilities it held open. Each year between 1950 and 1955 was devoted to a particular subtopic of the Advance's overall theme "Go—Make Disciples." In the flush of campaign enthusiasm, the General Assembly adopted the first million-dollar World Service budget. During the five-year period, the number of congregations increased by slightly more than ten percent and membership grew by roughly one-fourth.

The year 1950 seems an odd time for the movement to have oriented itself so strongly toward the future. The Church of God had not yet completely emerged from a divisive struggle, the wounds of which had not yet fully healed. A somewhat crippled movement launched the Mid-Century Advance.

In the second half of the 1940s a controversy had racked the movement. At the center of concern was the fear that the Church of God had organized and centralized itself to the point that it had become one of the very denominations we claimed to be protesting. Along with this, some expressed the fear that we had compromised our teaching on Christian unity and holy living. Charges and countercharges flew back and forth. The characters of good people were called into question. A small-scale schism tore the body of Christ. The movement's confidence staggered.

I am intrigued by the thought that Church of God people looked to a bright future in a moment when some must have wondered whether there would be a future at all. Maybe

48

they simply wanted to put on a brave face. Maybe some clever leaders decided that the Advance was a program that would get the church's mind off its problems. Maybe, but I don't think so.

The Mid-Century Advance expressed the movement's hope as it looked to the future. But hope that is not grounded in history is nothing but the hype of "pie-in-the-sky." Real hope occurs in the midst of history, in the midst of our everyday successes and shortcomings. As Walter Brueggemann observes, history without hope produces the despair that will kill our spirits. But hope severed from history is a narcotic (1987:3). Real hope takes account of the events of our lives and then says, "Nevertheless . . ." But hope's "nevertheless" never denies the circumstances of our lives.

I do not know for certain, but I want to believe that the men and women who planned the Advance did so only after taking account of the bitter controversy that still swirled about them. If that is the case, then these people displayed the Christian virtue of hope.

Chapter 2 Note

*Those interested in a fuller treatment of Jackson's life may wish to read James E. Massey's, *Raymond S. Jackson, A Portrait*, p. 1967, from which biographical details were taken for this essay.

OVERS OF TRUTH

"A cordial invitation is given to all lovers of the truth to this general convocation of the children of God, on the campground at the Trumpet Home in the northeast part of the city." So opened the announcement for the June 1902 camp meeting at Moundsville, West Virginia. What does it mean to be "lovers of the truth?"

"The truth" is an important theme in sermons and songs of the early Church of God movement. A songbook published by the Gospel Trumpet Company in 1907 carried the title, *Truth in Song.* People sometimes concluded testimonies published in *the Gospel Trumpet* with a closing such as "your brother and sister, saved and sanctified through the truth." An often quoted New Testament text was John 17:17—"Sanctify them in thy *truth*; thy word is *truth*."* Clearly our early preachers, writers, and poets connected the movement with "truth."

But we must pursue the matter further. After all, "lovers of the truth" is not much more than a slogan. When the *Gospel Trumpet* invited all "lovers of the truth" to Moundsville Camp Meeting, what was meant by "truth"? And what did it mean to love the truth?

We must state right away that early Church of God preachers and writers thought that the truth was something in which people ought to believe. To believe "the truth," however, was only the beginning. By exhorting men and women to believe the truth, the movement's leaders did not intend the reduction of Christianity to a series of belief statements or conduct an exercise in logic-chopping. The real essence of Christianity was *experiencing* the truth, and that lay beyond belief. C. W. Naylor captured this idea in the song "It Is True within My Heart," published in *Select Hymns* (1911). The chorus reads

> "I have read within the Bible
> What his favor will impart;
> And, Oh Glory! I have proved it,
> Now "tis true within my heart."

The truth of the Bible was to be *believed*, but the *experience* of the truth caused the soul to sing "Oh Glory!" early Church of God people thus sang their conviction that the truth was something better experienced than believed.

Connected with the idea that truth is experienced was a second important notion about truth. Knowledge of the truth, says much early Church of God writing, is progressive. That is one reason we have resisted the temptation to tie ourselves down to creeds or doctrinal statements; they set in concrete that which is historical and therefore subject to change. A phrase commonly used to describe the changing knowledge of the truth was that "more light" was to be had on a particular point.

Before D. S. Warner died in December, 1895, he published some articles on divine healing. He said that the use of "naturally occurring remedies" (e.g., herb teas, poultices, and so forth) was consistent with the practice of divine healing. But very shortly after Warner's death, his editorial successor, E. E. Byrum, wrote articles in which he argued that the saints could use no medicines, natural or otherwise. The difference between his position and Warner's Byrum explained by saying that his late departed brother did not have all the light that was to be had on this subject. Byrum could make that judgment because of the movement's idea that knowledge of the truth is progressive.

All of this suggests that when "lovers of the truth" were

invited to Moundsville Camp Meeting in 1902, they were really being invited to come along on a journey. The movement invited others to experience the truth and thereby risk the possibility that their knowledge of the truth might expand. Such an invitation places heavy burdens on those who would join such a pilgrimage.

The pilgrimage of truth that is the "Church of God way" is a journey "from light unto light." That means we will not write down as truth for the ages that which we "know." Knowledge of the truth is progressive; more light is still to be had. These days we think we will be less fearful, and more secure, if we can just come to definitive statements "once and for all." But that is a policy born of fear and quite contrary to the spirit of Jesus, who taught us not to fear the truth. It also contradicts what *we* once said and experienced of the truth.

Our pilgrimage of truth exacts heavy demands of us in a second way. If the knowledge of truth is progressive, as we have said, then we will not be able to use violence and coercion for its defense. For those false weapons are better suited to rigid, fixed positions, inappropriate for pilgrims journeying from light to light. Our pilgrimage of truth requires us to live open to new light—even when it shines from unanticipated quarters.

Important questions remain. Are we so committed to being truthful people that we will walk the pilgrimage of truth when some of our own ideas cannot withstand the penetrating light of honest inquiry? We have asked others to walk in this way. Should we not ask ourselves to walk in it also?

"Lovers of the truth are invited."

TRUTH: MORE PURSUED THAN CAPTURED

A building on the west side of Sixty-eighth Avenue in Portland, Oregon houses the Warner Pacific College Library. Constructed at an estimated cost of $125,000 in the early 1950s, the building occupies the loveliest site on the

53

campus; birch and maple trees surround it, and fir-covered Mount Tabor rises immediately to the north.

Warner Pacific students, and probably some faculty members and administrators, commonly refer to it as "the library." But it is not *the* library. Dedicated on November 24, 1954, the Warner Pacific College library carries the name and thus honors the college's first dean, Dr. Otto F. Linn. So references to the library there ought to be to *Linn* Library. Especially on this, the eve of the fiftieth anniversary year of the founding of Warner Pacific (originally, Pacific Bible College), we ought to remember, or perhaps introduce, Otto Linn.

Linn was born to Swedish-American parents at Falun, Kansas, in 1887. Converted in 1905, young Otto came to the Gospel Trumpet Company and offered his services in the publishing work. From 1910 to 1912 he worked with D. O. Teasley in the New York City missionary home. During the years 1912-1923 Linn served pastorates in Oklahoma and Kansas. He followed this with two years of missionary work in Denmark and Norway.

While active in church work, Linn also pursued formal education. He took B.A. and M.A. degrees from Phillips University in Oklahoma. In the 1930s he completed the Ph.D. program at the University of Chicago. His major professor there was Edgar J. Goodspeed, one of the foremost American authorities on the New Testament and the translator of *The Bible: An American Translation.*

Linn became the first Church of God minister to earn an academic doctorate. His generation of leaders in the movement included Russell Byrum, C. E. Brown, and a somewhat younger member, Adam W. Miller. All of these people sought to bring scholarship to bear on the life of the Church of God. Brown was a church historian, Byrum a theologian; Miller and Linn worked in New Testament studies. Linn was a consummate scholar in this field, a judgment born out by his selection as a member of the translation committee that produced the Revised Standard Version of the New Testament.

Otto F. Linn

Otto F. Linn (1887-1965) was the first Church of God minister to earn the Ph.D. degree. In addition to serving as Dean of Pacific Bible College, Linn also taught New Testament there and, earlier, at Anderson College. He pastored congregations in Oklahoma and Maryland and served as a missionary to Norway and Denmark. His major publications are his three-volume commentary, *Studies in the New Testament,* and a commentary on the Gospel According to John.

Linn was one of those people in the movement who have been captured by our notion that the truth may be pursued more than possessed. He firmly opposed authoritarian control of some minds by other minds. He encouraged people to frame their own careful, informed conclusions.

Three sentences from his introduction to *Studies in the New Testament, Vol. III* emphasize the point: "If this brief study is disturbing enough to provoke independent thinking and research, the author will feel amply rewarded for his efforts. Even ministers may be too prone to let others do their thinking. Such an intellectual indifference contributes to the tyranny of an opinion that may have established itself" (p. 10).

Linn did not insist that everyone agree with him, but he did want his readers to think for themselves. He also expected them to be as tolerant of his ideas as he was of theirs. In that last attitude rings the note of humility that characterized the life of this gentle scholar.

Otto Linn taught at Anderson College during the first half of the 1930s. From 1936 to 1942 he pastored the congregation at Dundalk, Maryland. Along the way he managed to write a fine three-volume commentary on the New Testament. Much of that work appeared as serialized lessons in the *Gospel Trumpet* during 1940-41.

In addition to his contributions to the adult Sunday school curriculum, he later published a commentary on the Gospel of John. In 1942 he moved to Portland to assume the position of dean at Pacific Bible College, a position he held until forced into retirement by Parkinson's Disease in April 1955. Ten years later he died.

Linn and some of the leaders of his generation forced the movement to ground itself in the whole Bible instead of relying only on a narrow reading of Daniel and the Revelation. They sounded a note of scholarship and insisted with quiet determination that we begin to read and understand the Bible in light of that scholarship. They introduced us to the realm of learning.

Furthermore, they reminded us of something we know but

have a sorry tendency to forget: we do not have all the truth. They remembered that better than many of us, and so they searched for truth where it might be found. Their relentless searching teaches us another lesson: truth is something of which we still need never be afraid.

THE CHURCH AND EDUCATION

In 1903 God called Albert F. Gray into the ministry. A seer would hardly have envisioned seventeen-year-old Albert, who had completed the eighth grade only a year earlier, as a future college president.

Gray only recently had moved to Spokane from Grand Forks, North Dakota. There his widowed mother and his brothers and sisters had entered the Church of God movement. They continued their active membership once they relocated in the Pacific Northwest. In 1904 the Grays and other Church of God people began worshiping in the newly constructed Spokane missionary home. The Spokane home quickly became the center of ministerial activity and training in the Inland Empire.

Along with practical training in such ministerial skills as visitation and literature distribution, young ministers like Albert could take courses during the winter months at the Spokane home. G. W. Bailey taught Bible geography, Bible history, music theory, and sight singing. O. A. Burgess expanded the curriculum after his arrival in 1907. He developed a correspondence course for ministers that first was offered in 1915. The thirty-six week program was rigorous; students were expected to read one book per day, Sundays excepted, during the course. Burgess' correspondence course helped Albert prepare for the ministry.

Gray's study also included correspondence work with the New York Bible Institute. The idea of offering ministerial training at Church of God missionary homes mushroomed after 1915. In addition to the Bible training schools at Spokane and New York, the Kansas City and Anderson homes opened training schools. The New York Institute's course of study was particularly impressive. Its correspondence courses were prepared by such noteworthy people as D. O. Teasley, G. P. Tasker and A. D. Khan, the last two being university-trained themselves. Such people were A. F. Gray's teachers through the correspondence courses they constructed.

The premise of the Bible training schools was, of course, that candidates for the ministry would benefit from education. School leaders viewed learning as an asset to ministry. In these early educational ventures, the movement served as sponsor and context; education was connected to the church. For example, C. J. Blewitt was listed as the *pastor* of the New York home in which the institute resided in 1919. Church and educational ventures were tied together by very short strings. That does not mean, however, that none opposed the institutes.

The schools in New York and Kansas City eventually closed. The Spokane school relocated in Boise, Idaho, and later in Seattle before suspending operations in the early 1920s. To fill the Northwest's educational vacuum, Pacific Bible College was launched in 1937. Over the years its mission enlarged as it grew into the institution we know as Warner Pacific College. The same can be said of each of the Church of God movement's liberal arts colleges. While their missions have grown, each school remains closely tied to the church.

The relationship between colleges and church ought to be close and reciprocal. Why? The answer may not be obvious. Indeed, some people make the opposite point—that church groups should not sponsor colleges, that church and college both would be happier if they went their separate ways.

A Christian liberal arts college is a difficult enterprise. Several traditions join themselves in these particular kinds of institutions. From the liberal arts comes the idea that knowledge is freedom; freedom from superstition, fear, obscurantism. But freedom is not its own end, and neither rationality nor learning of itself makes free people good. Therefore, the freedom gained through instruction in the

A. F. Gray

A. F. Gray (1886-1969) was a largely self-taught minister-educator in the Church of God. Gray's formal education for the ministry included the correspondence course of the New York missionary home's Bible institute. He also took courses at the institute sponsored by the Spokane home. Eventually he became the founding president of Pacific Bible College (later, Warner Pacific College). One of the truly distinguished ministers of the Church of God, Gray presided over the General Ministerial Assembly for many years. He also taught theology at Pacific Bible College, his major book being *Christian Theology*.

liberal arts must be offered some direction. Christianity and the church offer those who would be free the ancient wisdom that will guide free men and women in its use.

Christians know that freedom is a tool to be employed in the service of God and neighbor. The liberal arts need Christianity's reminder that freedom is not an end in itself. The church needs the liberal arts' reminder that inquiry and discovery are essential to human existence, that humans must be free for that quest. College and church thus need each other as mutual reminders that the completion of their tasks is assisted by the presence of the other.

The people who founded the Bible institutes at Spokane, Kansas City, Anderson, and New York did not envision their tiny enterprises growing into Christian liberal arts colleges. Their goals were much more utilitarian. But their instinct for education in the context of the church endures.

A DIALOGICAL CHURCH

Charles Hodge, longtime professor and president of Princeton Seminary during the nineteenth century, once remarked that during his tenure there had been not so much as a single new idea at Princeton. As for the future, Hodge promised that no novel thoughts would see the light of day during his stewardship of the institution. For Hodge, education in seminary and, presumably, in the church was a matter of indoctrination. Such a notion of education assumes that the church's teachers must indoctrinate, conduct catechism classes.

Two events occur in association with the World Conference of the Church of God that suggest that the movement understands the church quite differently than people like Charles Hodge. At World Conferences in Anderson (1980), Nairobi (1983) and Seoul (1987) people from around the globe have met in the World Forum and the International Dialogue on Doctrinal Issues. These events do not seek the indoctrination of anyone. No one attends in order to be told by another what to think or believe. New ideas are not suppressed in these meetings. Quite to the contrary, all participants have the opportunity to contribute to the group's conversation from their own perspectives. Since no single person can possibly view the whole, it stands to reason that the unique perspectives of Forum and Dialogue participants will be perceived by some other participants as new ideas.

Such a dialogical process is critical if we are to be the movement of God's Spirit that we have claimed to be. For more than a century we have said that we have "no creed but the Bible." Already that puts us on the opposite side of the fence from people like Charles Hodge, who did not particularly care for the no-creed-but-the-Bible people of his day. Moreover, through the decade of the 1920s several events occurred that illustrate the movement's opposition to anything like Hodge's viewpoint.

During the 1920s the General Ministerial Assembly (as it then was known) considered a resolution that identified 1924 as the end point of a period of time in which the "standard literature" of the movement was said to have been produced. In effect, the proposed resolution made new ideas inconsequential at best and inconsiderable at worst. The principle target of the resolution was R. R. Byrum's *Christian Theology*, published in 1925. The Assembly rejected the resolution. Later that same decade Byrum was exonerated in a heresy trial wherein he was accused, among other things, of teaching material not in agreement with our so-called standard literature. Criticizing this same "standard literature mentality," George Tasker wrote from Calcutta in 1924: "Appeals to 'what the church believes' and to 'the fathers,' when these expressions are used in narrow restrictive sense . . . , sound altogether too much like the language of the apostasy, when men began to defend their own ecclesiastical views instead of trying them constantly and ruthlessly by the Word and Spirit of the Lord."[2]

All of this suggests that World Forum and Theological Dialogue participants are very much the heirs of those in the movement who would not tolerate the end of serious new ideas and thinking in 1924. To suppress new ideas would simultaneously signal the end of meaningful conversation. What would there be to talk about?

Even more important, to standardize ideas would have helped to bring an end to the idea that the church is a verb more than noun. We have called ourselves a movement in part to reject that static quality of institutions that comes through standardization. Instead we have emphasized activity. Indeed, among the church's most important activities is talk among ourselves, not idle conversation but serious dialogue about the implications of Scripture and the movement's historical journey that now call us to action. One may in fact think of the church precisely as that conversation.

In this view events like the World Forum and International Dialogue on Doctrinal Issues are not extraneous opportunities for people to let off steam. They are, rather, among the most important expressions of the Church of God way of being the church.

ONE LESSON WELL TAUGHT

The agency we know today as the Board of Christian Education first saw the light of day during the 1923 Anderson Camp Meeting. That June the General Ministerial Assembly, itself only six years old, created the "Board of Religious Education and Sunday Schools." The board lived through some lean early years. For example, no paid staff implemented board actions; they had to do their own work. Among the charter members of that hardworking board was a thirty-four year old woman named Bessie Hittle Byrum.

Bessie Hittle was born January 4, 1889 in Greenville, Ohio. Years later, after her conversion, she came to work for the Gospel Trumpet Company. Soon she found her niche in the editorial department. There she became the company's first editor of children's quarterlies and also wrote church school lesson commentaries. In 1916 she married Russell R. Byrum, then managing editor of the Trumpet Company. Both of them served on the faculty, she part-time, at Anderson Bible Training School when its first classes convened the next fall. She continued in this post for fourteen years.

In 1927 Byrum was elected president of the "Sunday School Board," as it was widely known. She threw her considerable natural ability and energies into that assignment. In the process she spurred the Church of God movement into an era of considerable development in the field of Christian education. The board's work covered all aspects of Christian education—Sunday schools, vacation Bible school, curriculum, youth work, and teacher training programs. One may look at back issues of the *Trumpet* and discover articles by Bessie Byrum on all of those topics and more.

Byrum presided over the board during the time when the Trumpet Company switched its Sunday school curriculum from a base in the Uniform Lesson Outlines to what were called graded lesson plans. She enthusiastically supported this change. She preferred the latter because its lessons were planned with reference to student age levels and learning abilities. She believed this to be a great advance over lessons that required "Sunday scholars" (as they often were called) to master a body of content, whether or not they could comprehend it.

Students mattered first to Byrum. Her published talks on teacher preparation breathe her concern that teachers begin their lesson planning with a consideration of their students. As she put matters in a 1923 *Trumpet* article, "Sunday school teacher, you have a big job. You cannot hope for greater success by giving just the Sunday school hour than the pastor can have by limiting his work to a sermon on Sunday. Personal work is needed" (1923:7). Sunday school teachers, argued Bessie, should consider themselves the pastors of their classes.

Bessie Byrum saw in the Sunday school the church's greatest opportunity for growth. Anyone could start a Sunday school anywhere. Children enrolled in them gave workers access to unsaved parents. Given the prevalence of teen-age conversions, Sunday schools were the likeliest place for those conversions to occur. Sunday schools also developed strong Christian character. As Byrum put the matter, "Of individuals saved in a revival, those who have been Sunday school attendants are three times more likely to be stable than those who were not" (1923:13-14).

Bessie Byrum did more than write about Christian education. For forty years she served as church school superintendent at Park Place Church of God in Anderson. Her pleasant combination of common sense ("Better one lesson [on Sunday] taught well than many poorly taught") and innovation (the congregation's first vacation Bible school was held under her leadership) guided the course of Christian education there for four decades.

In consideration of all her contributions to the life of the movement, Anderson College conferred on Bessie Byrum an honorary doctorate in 1967, two years after her retirement— at age seventy-six. She died in May of 1971. Those who have grown up in the educational ministry of the Church of God movement have felt her influence whether or not they ever were privileged to know her. For, as her obituary said in a mastery of understatement, "She was a remarkable woman."

FLAME OF THE FOREST

Throughout the Caribbean there grows a flowering tree known variously by some as "Spathodia" or "African Tulip"; others call it the "Flame of the Forest." By whichever name it is called this tree graces the island countryside with beauty and a natural elegance.

Amidst such loveliness Amy Lopez was born at Chapelton, Clarendon, Jamaica in 1894. Learning and wisdom graced her childhood years. Her education at Wolmer's Girls School fired in her a desire for knowledge and a love of the English language. In those same years Lopez experienced conversion. From that point in her life she became a disciple of the one she was accustomed to call the Master.

As a young woman Lopez came to know that her life's vocation was teaching. She left Jamaica in 1923 to attend the University of Wisconsin, then enjoying a reputation as

Amy Lopez

Amy Lopez (1894-1971) taught English at Anderson College for twenty-three years. A native of Jamaica, Lopez was converted as a young woman. Teaching was her great love. She was possessed of such natural grace that her former students often begin reminiscing about her with comments about her gracefulness and polite, elegant manners.

one of the brightest lights of American higher education. In 1927 Lopez joined the faculty of Anderson College as a professor in the English department and dean of women.

In those days Anderson reached far and wide to draw upon the best talent and wisdom of the movement. President Morrison had come from Delta, Colorado, Dean Olt from Cincinnati. Now Amy Lopez arrived from Jamaica. She interrupted her teaching at the college twice, once to pursue an M.A. in English at Columbia University. Later she studied at Oxford.

George Bernard Shaw's Professor Henry Higgins made the ironic charge that Americans had not spoken English for years. Tall and possessed of the kind of dignity that commands through its winsomeness, Amy Lopez taught AC and Jamaican students the King's English—with a Jamaican lilt. She taught young men and women more than English, however. Her students also learned about compassion and an abiding love for humanity, qualities that found their way into her courses because they were among her many virtues.

Had you the opportunity to ask Amy Lopez her motive for teaching, she would have said, "Teaching here means coming in vital relationship with young people whose lives are characterized by strong conviction and deep self-denial. But, above all and inclusive of all I have said is the fact that in teaching I have the opportunity of following the Master whose ministry was largely a teaching ministry" (1941:7).

In 1950 Lopez returned to her Jamaican home. For over twenty years she continued the ministry that followed her Master. Some of those years she spent as a teacher or an administrator. Another part of that time she served as a senior inspector of children's schools for the Jamaican Office of Education. Her last assignment found her teaching at Mandeville High School. In all this she faithfully served out her ministerial vocation. Her character permitted no alternatives.

One October day in 1971, a taxi carrying Lopez and several other passengers was involved in a multi-vehicle accident. Gravely injured, she was taken to a nearby hospital where she died two days later.

From the time Lopez entered the ministry, she served her Lord with strength and discipline. People in North America and around the world were drawn to the natural elegance of her warm spirituality. Such lives are gifts to us from God, meant to light our path.

EDUCATION THAT MODELS

On a Kansas homestead five miles west of the Santa Fe Trail, Irene Smith was born in 1909. Life being very hard there, her parents moved their family to the softer life of Oklahoma in 1913. Four-year-old Irene rode to her new home in a covered wagon.

Neither church nor school were to be found near the Smith homestead. So Smith's early education came in the form of a children's library compiled of books written by early Church of God writers. Her uncle Fred had met D. S. Warner in a brush arbor meeting and there had stood for the truth, hence the family's selection of Church of God authors. Books could not substitute for a real school, however, so eighteen-year-old Otto Linn was brought in to teach. Linn did more than run a school. He also looked after the children. When illness quarantined the Smith family, young Otto was the one to go for groceries. When Smith was six, Linn persuaded the family to attend a nearby camp meeting. Elsie Egermeier held children's meetings there, and under her winsome teaching young Irene dedicated her life to God. Irene Smith's Christian education had begun.

Over the years Smith's life further intertwined itself with the church's educational ministry. Sometimes this meant additional academic work. She took degrees at Anderson College, Oberlin School of Theology, and the University of Southern California. Adam Miller saw to it that the Board of Christian Education gave her an assignment for which she was paid the magnificent sum of twenty-five dollars a week. Primarily she worked as a professor of Christian education

67

Irene Smith Caldwell

Irene Smith Caldwell (1909-1979) taught at four different Church of God institutions of higher education. Christian education was her field of academic expertise and her life's work, beginning with her assignment at the Board of Christian Education of the Church of God. The author of numerous books and articles, Dr. Caldwell gave tirelessly to the educational ministry of the Church of God.

in Church of God educational institutions: twenty-two years at Warner Pacific, seven at Anderson School of Theology and another five at Warner Southern College. Smith also taught at Warner Memorial University in Eastland, Texas. In addition to her teaching assignment there, she was minister to youth and children.

Just prior to moving to Warner Pacific in 1945, Irene married Mack Caldwell, a widower with seven children, all of them teen-agers.

Christian education is not merely what the church does once it has its theology straight. Sunday schools are not indoctrination centers. Irene Smith Caldwell knew these facts and much more. She saw beyond the artificial confines of narrowly framed expertise. For her, Christian education and the Sunday school were but one form of the church's educational ministry. And how could it have been otherwise? Think of the way Otto Linn exemplified for young Irene and her family the church and the Christian life. Such simple, eloquent testimonies already began forming Irene's conception of the church and Christian education. So, for example, she simply could not understand, years later, how Christian education would *not* be connected to the church's mission or to Christian convictions about peace.

Irene Smith Caldwell died on April 4, 1979. Her life of discipleship had carried her to many fields of service. But in each of those fields her work was sustained by a continuing vision of the teacher's role: "Bring out the best in your students." Dr. Caldwell did not simply teach that dictum. She modeled it in her own life. As such she modeled what it means to be a member of the body of Christ. Is that not after all the church's educational ministry?

SCHOOLS OF WISDOM

Before the days of colleges and the seminary, men and women called to the ministry of the Church of God often received training in one of the numerous missionary homes of the movement. These homes varied considerably in style and activities. All the homes engaged in evangelistic work and housed gospel workers, evangelists, and colporteurs who busily labored at spreading the movement's message. Beyond evangelism, some homes specialized in rescue mission work. Others focused attention on a particular immigrant group, as in the case of the Germans at St. Joseph, Michigan, and the Scandinavians at St. Paul Park, Minnesota. The great majority of homes were led by white ministers, but at least one of them, the missionary home in Pittsburgh, Pennsylvania, was operated by, and served the needs of, black ministers and gospel workers. The Pittsburgh home's principal leader was a man named R. J. Smith.

Today we would call R. J. Smith one of the movement's "pioneers," for indeed he broke the trails taken by many others who followed after him. Originally joining company with the Church of God in the South, Smith served as a pastor and evangelist for more than thirty years until his death in 1925. He built up the congregation at Paulson Avenue church in Pittsburgh and served some of his most rewarding years there. But he also knew controversy and the dangerous consequences of bold preaching. Once, after a particularly fearless sermon in Charleston, South Carolina, Smith found himself being used for target practice by a local gunman.

R. J. Smith impressed others with his ability to get people to join seriously in the work of the church. That ability is one of the characteristics of good leadership. Smith's colleagues in the ministry must have recognized that quality and others in him, for he was elected Chair of the General Ministerial Assembly of the National Association of the Church of God from 1917 to 1923. He was the first such chairperson, and it surely must count as a sign of respect to be the first called upon to serve a new organization in such a capacity.

Leaders like R. J. Smith require the presence of certain virtues in their lives. A virtue is the quality that enables a person or object to fulfill its purpose. For example, the keen

R. J. Smith

R. J. Smith (1864-1925) served as the first chairperson of the General Assembly of the National Association of the Church of God. Among the leading ministers of the Church of God, Smith superintended the missionary home in Pittsburgh, Pennsylvania.

71

edge of a knife blade enables it to cut, and a dull knife is useless because it cannot do what a knife must. So we might say that a dull knife has lost its virtue. People also have virtues, and people cast into particular roles may need to cultivate specific virtues that enable them to fulfill those roles. When one thinks of leadership, virtues like courage, patience, and constancy come to mind—along with those inevitable Christian virtues—faith, hope, and love.

How do leaders, who often start out as ordinary people, come to possess such virtues? Surely they begin in the gracious presence of the Holy Spirit. But even after such gifting, the virtues must be developed through exercising them. That was another especially important function of the missionary homes. They served as training grounds for leadership. To be sure, people called to ministry came to the homes for training in the techniques necessary for pastoral and evangelistic work. But learning the virtues requisite for leadership is more than mastering a set of skills or memorizing a series of "action-steps." Leadership requires that our characters be formed in ways that embody the virtues that enable leaders to fulfill their purpose. Since that is the case, the missionary homes needed to be, and often were, schools of wisdom. R. J. Smith's ministerial labor is but one splendid example of many people who received training in the virtues at the missionary homes.

Now it is the case that all Christians are called to ministry, some of whom are lay and others ordained. Thus it follows that the congregations in which we gather, and the colleges and seminary in which we educate people, should have something of this dimension of the school of wisdom wherein the virtues necessary for ministry are formed. In the form of the missionary homes this notion served the movement well.

Chapter 3 Note

*Emphasis added.

Love 4

GOD'S CHISEL

They were just babies, Mary and Martha Hunter. The two little girls became ill in August of 1903, during the camp meeting at Claypool, Indiana. Word of their worsening condition spread, and soon all of the saints in the camp were praying for God's healing of these twin sisters.

Only a year earlier Mary and Martha had been born to Nora S. and Clarence Hunter. Before her marriage, Nora had participated in a wide variety of evangelistic efforts. She had left her adopted home in southeastern Kansas to join Dr. and Mrs. S. G. Bryant in their evangelistic ministry. By 1893 she was in Grand Junction, Michigan. Nora preached the reformation truths on the deck of the *Floating Bethel*, and she teamed with Lena Shoffner in evangelizing Maryland.

After her marriage to Clarence in 1896, Nora continued her strong evangelistic ministry. In order to provide for his young family, Clarence occasionally supplemented his own ministerial labor with secular work. But for Nora the work of the church remained a consuming passion. These were two dedicated servants who brought their babies with them to Yellow Creek Lake meeting.

Despite the fervent prayers of all those gathered on the grounds, the little girls died a few days after their first birthday. Their graves can be found in a small cemetery a

The Hunter Family

Clarence and Nora Hunter, their children: Paul and the infant daughters Mary and Martha. Nora Hunter (1873-1951) was one of the outstanding leaders in the Church of God movement. She was a minister and evangelist whose most noteworthy achievement was the founding of the National Foreign and Home Missionary Society of the Church of God (later, Women of the Church of God), an organization which she served as president for its first sixteen years.

movement. But the seeds of what he and others had sown continued to reap a bitter harvest. So it is when we sin against love. But does not God's love stand even against our sins against love? Maybe even in this all-too-serious episode that is farcical, but for its sad consequences, there remains yet a hint of divine humor. Perhaps Robert Louis Stevenson was right when he wrote, "For the life of man upon this world of ours is a funny business. They talk of the angels weeping, but I think they must more often be holding their sides, as they look on" (Stevenson 1974:427).

HANDSHAKE RELIGION

In 1895 two Church of God evangelists traveled to Federalsburg, Maryland. Nora Hunter and Lena Shoffner held forth in revival meetings there for six weeks. They sang and prayed; they exhorted mightily. But no spiritual harvest resulted from their labors. So one night they announced that if nobody was saved in the next meeting that service would conclude the revival. The next service arrived, and at its conclusion a man rose to give his heart to the Lord. Others followed and, in Hazel Neal's words, "A congregation was born overnight" (Neal 17).

Shoffner had been converted through the Warner evangelistic company's work in Missouri only five years earlier. Lena became one of the first members of the Carthage congregation. But her flaming spirit could not be confined to southwest Missouri. Her passion for the gospel eventually carried her on an evangelistic tour of England, concentrating particularly on the cities of London and Liverpool.

In 1903 Shoffner opened a revival in Oklahoma City. The nature of her gospel labor changed here, for she remained for the next eight years as the first regular Church of God pastor in that town. She also married Ed Mattheson. Together they served the church as Oklahoma pastors and evangelists until Lena's death at age sixty-eight in 1937.

Like many other Church of God preachers and evangelists, Lena Shoffner's spirit was forged in the fires of revivalism.

few miles west of the camp ground.

In 1903 the Church of God movement's theology of healing could not explain very satisfactorily the kind of calamity that struck Nora and Clarence Hunter. By then sickness had come to be regarded as the effect of one of four causes: (a) Satan, who wanted to afflict the soul of the one he made physically sick; (b) God, who wanted to chastise a sinner back to moral health; (c) sin, which led to its own disastrous consequences; or (d) the "sickness-unto-death," meaning that the afflicted person had come to that time appointed for each of us to die. But none of these explanations adequately accounted for the illness and deaths of two innocent babies.

The same year that Nora and Clarence were married a young man named Charles Wesley Naylor offered his services to the Gospel Trumpet Company. They accepted him and put him to work in the subscriptions department. Before long he was writing books and poetry set to music for the hymnals and songbooks published by the company. His many songs include "The Church's Jubilee," "Once Again We Come," "More Like Christ," "I Am the Lord's," and the beautiful "Spirit Holy."

Trumpet workers, even poets, labored at a variety of manual tasks when sweat and elbow grease were required. Naylor also did his share of heavy work. But an accident occurred while he worked setting up a large meeting tent, and Naylor sustained severe internal injuries. He never recovered and eventually was left bedfast and in unrelieved pain. God could not be blamed for the accident, but why wasn't Naylor healed? More than one person who knew of the case asked that question. Despite the fact that some came to Naylor's bedside to be anointed for healing by him, slanderous stories circulated about the poet's "hidden sin."

Naylor, too, wondered why God did not restore him to full physical health. A line from the song he wrote with Clarence Hunter, "God's way is best, I will not murmur," expresses the answer Naylor got to his question. From his pen also comes a sentence that enlarged our theology of healing, if only we will hear it: "Pain is God's chisel, with which he carves his image in the heart."

In our time and place, when we look for ways to avoid suffering at all cost, Naylor's words seem callous and only cold comfort. He did not say that we should seek pain, but when suffering visits us, we may also find God at work bringing to perfection a work already begun. Naylor's poetry, his books, and his life enable us to speak a word of consolation to others who have suffered in ways like Nora and Clarence Hunter—those who have lost a child in a senseless accident, those who have lost a spouse in a dreadful fight with cancer, those who see the morning's happiness evaporate in swift unimaginable loss. Charles Naylor gave words to the mystery that embraces suffering people of faith. He knew for them, and for us, that especially in those places, the God of heartache is at work, chiseling out the divine image with a wholeness, a *shalom*, a peace that passes all understanding.

THE GREAT NECKTIE CONTROVERSY

In the last years of the last decade of the nineteenth century, a group of ministers led by W. A. Haynes, W. J. Henry, E. G. Masters and others revised their teaching on sanctification. Like other holiness movement groups of that time, the Church of God movement had interpreted sanctification according to one side of John Wesley's thought, that popularized by Adam Clarke of commentary fame. In essence, this view said that God's grace operated twice in a person's life, initially at justification and subsequently at sanctification. The first work God does *for* us; the second is done *in* us.

One group deviated from this generally held doctrine and began teaching an interpretation in which sanctification was thought to take place at the same moment that persons were justified. Because these teachings were associated with Nicholas Zinzendorf, Wesley's sometime friend and theological opponent, the novel teaching soon acquired the label "Zin-

zendorfism." Because a part of Zinzendorf's teaching included the idea of "imputed" (but not real) sanctification, Zinzendorfism also became known by its opponents as the "anti-cleansing heresy."

The word *heresy* marks the serious nature of the controversy. More than theological subtleties were at stake; schism, the sin against unity, was in the air. In the aftermath of the tension-filled Moundsville Camp Meeting of 1899 a serious rupture indeed occurred. Some of the best preachers left the movement, but they never coalesced into a group. Some joined denominational churches or other groups such as the Disciples of Christ. Others found their way back into the fellowship of the Church of God movement. The movement's understanding of sanctification was not resolved, however, with the end of the anti-cleansing conflict.

In 1903 C. E. Orr published *Christian Conduct*. This little book focused the movement's attention on its practical expression of the doctrine of sanctification. Ever since Warner's early days as a holiness preacher, the outward form of the sanctified life had been the subject of numerous Church of God sermons. Orr's book put the matter in the spotlight. The recent debate over Zinzendorfism only served to narrow the beam of that light. Together, Orr's book and the earlier debate brought the question of appropriate Christian behavior to an incendiary point.

For men the necktie became the great watershed of practical sanctification. Wearing one signaled worldliness; forsaking the tie demonstrated holiness. It scarcely seems possible that such an innocent article of clothing threatened to divide a movement called to witness to Christian unity. The controversy seems ironically humorous, but the irony is almost too painful to endure. When Christians either threaten or, worse, act out self-division, they further rend Christ's seamless robe, and that scarcely seems a laughing matter. Whether ironic or tragic, C. E. Orr and many others broke fellowship with Christians who would not join in a resolution against wearing "the tie."

By 1915 Orr had repented his actions and rejoined the

Lena Shoffner Mattheson

Lena Shoffner Mattheson (1868-1937) was converted during meetings held by the Warner evangelistic company in Missouri in 1890. She was called into the ministry and served as an evangelist, pastor and missionary. Along with J. H. and Hattic Rupert, Shoffner traveled in Birkenhead, England in a wagon called the *Gospel Van.*

For their experience to have been so tempered was not uncommon, for the revival was a powerful force in nineteenth century American protestantism (and Catholicism, too, for that matter). Three of the most famous revival preachers in American history enjoyed their heyday during Lena Shoffner's ministry—D. L. Moody, Sam Jones, and Billy Sunday. The famous evangelist Charles G. Finney had died when Lena was still a young girl, but he had left a lasting impression on American preaching.

A fact worth noting is that some Church of God people criticized the methods of at least one of these celebrated preachers. The services at Billy Sunday's meetings concluded with an invitation to "hit the sawdust trail." (in those days the aisles of revival auditoriums, including those used by the Church of God, often were covered in sawdust.) As penitents came to the front of the auditorium, Sunday shook hands with them and said "God bless you." Then he turned these people over to workers who directed them to the first two rows of the auditorium where they filled out decision cards.

Gospel Trumpet writers attacked Sunday's "handshake religion," as they termed it. To their eyes it evidenced no godly sorrow, no signs of true repentance. Even more, it seemed to reflect a shallow conception of the Christian life. Early Church of God writers saw true revivals in moral terms. To them the Christian life could not be packaged in the routine of professional revivalism. They saw through the handshakes, cards, and general atmosphere of entertainment. Church of God critics of handshake religion envisioned conversion as a decision to follow Jesus wholeheartedly. The consequences of such a decision cannot be known the instant a person hits the sawdust trail. Their discovery requires a lifetime in imitation of the Master.

THE DEVIL IN POLITICS?

In 1904 Alton B. Parker challenged "His Accidency" Theodore Roosevelt for the presidency of the United States. Roosevelt had come by that label because he succeeded to the White House only after the assassination of William McKinley, a man T. R. once described as having the backbone of a chocolate eclair. In his race with Judge Parker, the colorful and popular Rough Rider galloped to an easy victory.

As the campaign wound its way through the autumn of 1904, readers of the Dano-Norwegian edition of the *Gospel Trumpet* came across an article titled "The Devil in Politics." The article did not actually recommend that Church of God people abstain from voting in the general election, but that seems to be its implication. Both parties claimed to have the best candidates yet, the article argued, such claims were logically impossible. But, probably of greater importance to protemperance Church of God people, neither Democrats nor Republicans had taken a hard stand against Demon Rum. To vote for candidates of either party therefore was to align oneself systemically with "wets" and deceivers. Should a Christian enter into such a tacit alliance? The article concluded by saying, "We will let every Christian answer this for himself."

Until 1928 "The Devil in Politics" was the strongest political statement in English, Scandinavian, or German language editions of the *Gospel Trumpet*. The English language paper, however, noted political items on a page called "Events and Comments" and later, "Observations of Our Times." A person reading the *Gospel Trumpet* during October of 1912 would have seen items in this section about Tsarist Russian designs on Persia, controversy over tolls charged to ships using the recently completed Panama Canal, concern for the nation's moral drift in the wake of the Roosevelt shooting, and fears that German canal construction on the Rhine River would seriously undermine Dutch commerce. One must conclude that the *Trumpet* wanted to inform but not influence its readers' politics.

As the 1928 presidential campaign unfolded, however, the *Trumpet* adopted a different policy. Two major issues of that campaign touched matters very close to the heart of the Church of God movement. In 1928 the Democrats nominated

Governor Al Smith for president. Smith was a "wet" concerning prohibition and a Roman Catholic, to boot. The fact that he was the governor of a large eastern state only increased his unacceptability in the eyes of many Church of God people. The *Gospel Trumpet* made these points perfectly clear. The paper's style had shifted, if only momentarily, from publishing political information to attempting to influence political decisions.

Some interesting observations rise out of these sketches of our past political attitudes. One must appreciate the sensitivity to systems apparent in the judgments of 1904. The people of that day seem to have seen, perhaps better than we, the organic, corporate nature of life in general. The people of that day clearly saw the systemic implications of an act like voting. But the recommendation to withdraw from politics that one infers in the implicit encouragement to refrain from voting is difficult to endorse. On the other hand, the willingness to state one's Christian convictions as a part of secular political debate as in the 1928 campaign is commendable.

Christians should exercise their freedom to speak on matters of public policy. But the Constitution guarantees the free speech of Christians no more than persons of any other religious persuasion. Church people can make of the Constitution no weapon to be used as a Christian club. The Christian art of persuasion can ultimately be found only in our witness—never in coercion, either mental or physical. Christians should participate in politics. But we often overlook the fact that all political activities are not appropriate to the church. The case may very well be that our strongest political influence will be through having good politics inside the church.

In the days before Constantine granted Christianity legal status in the Roman Empire, pagans were not nearly as impressed by what Christians said as they were by the kind of people they observed Christians to be and their way of living together, i.e., their politics. In a very important sense Christians cannot avoid politics. As the church they have a polity, they practice politics. Thus it is foolishness to wish for "unpoliticized" churches. The only question is the kind of politics we will practice. Will it be the politics of faction? Of self-interest? Or can it be the politics of a vision of the common good?

When the church rightly practices politics, which it does as it remembers the stories of Israel and its Lord, then it is in a position to witness in the American political arena. The politics of the church serves to remind the nation that it is neither eternal or the last, best hope of the world. The politics of the church reminds the nation of the identity of the world's true Lord. We can do that only by being the people of God who remember who they are and who they follow.

RELIGION AND WHITE BREAD

Sometimes we assume that our forefathers and foremothers in the Church of God thought and wrote only theology and doctrine. That is a serious historical mistake. To be sure, the major themes of their work focused on the unity and holiness of the church, the evangelization of sinners, and the divine healing of the sick. But early Church of God people also addressed themselves to ordinary, everyday life concerns.

In 1908 the Gospel Trumpet Company published a book by Thomas Nelson, *Home, Health and Success*. This edition had been translated from the Dano-Norwegian version, *Hjem, Helbred og Lykke*; not many people, in or out of the movement, were likely to read the original. The English translation proved to be popular, going through several printings.

Nelson wrote his book for the simple reason that he wanted people to be happy. The guide to that happiness Nelson had discovered in Nature's "immutable" and "unchangeable" laws, laid down by "the Creator himself" (1908:13). If we would but follow these laws, Nelson said, then happiness would be ours. It is very interesting that Nelson judged homes in terms of happy or unhappy rather than right or wrong. He offered his readers the chance to have a *happy* home rather than comfort them in the knowledge that they had a *right* home. Readers of his book in effect invited Nelson into their homes, where he could then make "helpful suggestions for their good and improvement as I see you most need in order to reap the sweet fruits of a happy home the remainder of your years" (12).

When Nelson was "invited" by readers into their homes, he went to their bedrooms first. Roughly the first fourth of Nelson's book dealt with marriage and sexuality. Nelson believed that shortly after marriage couples will awaken to the natural desire to "do their duty" and have children. In support of his belief Nelson quoted Theodore Roosevelt, who wanted high fertility levels so that the nation would always have a good supply of manhood. Nelson not only opposed contraception, he also attacked abortion as "cruel murder." With an insight ahead of his time, he encouraged mothers to love their children even before delivery.

Nelson reserved a large section of his book for instruction in matters of health. After a brief lesson in physiology, he launched a discussion in which he criticized white bread. This he followed with instructions on how to make good bread: the coarser the flour, the better the bread. Indeed, Nelson's general rule about food was the simpler the fare the better. He recommended only two drinks—milk and water, and he suggested that foods were healthier the closer they were to a raw state—even eggs. Nelson discussed the quantity as well as quality of food his readers ought to eat. He quoted *Home and Health*: "As many lives have been destroyed by gluttony as by drunkeness" (372).

What has religion to do with white bread? Why bother with questions about diet and business? What does Christianity have to do with political questions such as how much municipal treasury money is budgeted for playgrounds for inner-city children? Nelson commented on all of these subjects and more. What was the connection he saw between them and the "mighty reformation sweeping o'er the land?"

Implicit in Nelson's book is the belief that Christianity

cannot be summed up in a series of doctrinal statements. It is a way of life more than a code of belief. Sure, a few of his ideas are odd, and he draws upon some of the quackery of his age. But the idea that Christianity will influence our home, our health—even our politics and economics—is not foolishness. Except in the eyes of this world.

INCLUDING POSTUM?

The late John A. Morrison, first president of Anderson College, liked to tell a story about an elderly saint who frequently testified at East Prairie, Missouri Camp Meeting. The saint always testified to the same experience: "I am saved and sanctified from all forms of hot drinks; *and that includes Postum!*" The early Church of God holiness code prohibited "stimulants" such as coffee and tea. Postum, a beverage made from roasted grain, became the approved substitute, resembling coffee, however, only in that the former is hot, liquid, and brown.

The phrase "sanctified *from*" is extremely interesting, for it is a negative definition. The Missouri saint's definition of sanctification as "from" adopts the same negative tone as the following list, titled "Some Things You Ought Not Do," taken from an early *Gospel Trumpet*: "Do not forsake; Do not let your thoughts be wandering and your words overflowing; Do not spit on the floor in a home or in the meeting-house." How was it that we often chose to define holiness in terms of what Christians did *not* do? Of course we also sometimes explained sanctification positively. In the first years of the movement's life, sanctification signified the presence of godly love and unity. But over the years the tendency seems to have been to talk about holiness more as the absence of sin than the presence of love.

Along with this negative definition of holiness some people in the movement displayed an alarming tendency to consider abstinence from certain foods, beverages, forms of entertainment, and the like as badges of holiness. In some lectures delivered at the School of Theology in its early days, C. E.

Brown discerned two different attitudes toward the practice of such abstinence, which he called "ascetic disciplines" (1954). These disciplines, Brown said, could be considered either badges of holiness or means of discipline. Badges lead to religious pride. But by means, in the grace of God, we advance in holiness. Our character begins to conform to Christ's. Brown followed up his distinction with a strong appeal for our understanding of ascetic disciplines as means to the end of holiness.

C. E. Brown's distinction made a very important point. Badges of holiness have a way of supporting our pride in a manner that means of discipline never could. Although writing about a very different subject, George Lindbeck reinforces the idea that even the holiest of Christians possesses no warrant for pride or arrogance. "All human beings are toddlers, whether Peter or Paul, or the veriest infant in Christ. The decisive question regarding them is whether the language they have begun to learn by hearing is that of Jesus Christ, that of true humanity, or something else. . . . In any case, it is ridiculous for Christians to boast. They are like infants mouthing scraps of Shakespeare or the *Principia Mathematica*, parrot-like, by rote. Only occasionally do they have inklings of the meanings of the words they utter" (1984:61). As the Apostle Paul said, "May I never boast, except in the cross." (Gal. 6:14, NIV).

Many of us can name men or women who truly deserve to be called saints. I think of one person in particular, a frail, elderly woman with a bright eye that gave evidence of her alert, inquisitive mind. Well into her nineties she could be found in her customary pew, patiently listening and considering how better to follow her Master. She was sanctified, but not only *from*. She followed the way of holiness, but never boasted. She was quite aware that she, like all of us, could barely understand the meaning of what we confess with our lips. Such is the awareness of the sanctified.

RESPONSIBILITIES OF THE HEART

The Archives of the Church of God hold a revealing file of sad correspondence about one of the movement's little-known ministries, the old people's homes at Anderson and at St. Paul Park, Minnesota. Those homes tell us something important about the kind of people we were.

Sebastian Michels, an early "come-outer," started our interest in care for the elderly. Although opposed by those who thought ministry meant only preaching, Michels operated a home for the aged at South Haven, Michigan for twenty-five years. In 1907 the "Church of God Old People's Home of the Northwest" incorporated in Washington County, Minnesota. Construction began that same year on the home in Anderson. The saints started building the old people's home there before they put up the auditorium. What priorities might that sequence indicate?

The Anderson home was managed as a department of the Gospel Trumpet Company. Although intended to be self-supporting, the home often depended on subsidies from the publishing work. In 1921 a third of the Gospel Trumpet Company's benevolence budget—twelve thousand dollars—went to the support of the home. The load on company resources increased in 1920 when the St. Paul Park home also came under the control of the company. It closed in 1928, nearly ten years before the Anderson home experienced the same fate.

What did the homes expect of the men and women who wanted to live there? What did the managers consider as important information about prospective residents? The questions on their application forms offer some interesting answers to these questions: "What is your age?" "Are you white or colored?" "Are you destitute?" "Are you able to do work?" "Do you enjoy salvation?" "Do you belong to any secret orders?" "Do you use tobacco in any form?" "Are you willing to obey and conform to the rules and regulations of the home?" Three references also were required of each applicant.

Any reader of the letters attached to many of these yellowing applications will sense the loneliness and fear of some of their writers. Fannie Andriot, a widow from Hall, Montana, wanted to enter the Anderson home in 1926. The year is significant for, remember, the Social Security Act was not passed until 1935. Mrs. Andriot, in other words, lacked the monthly check that benefits the elderly in our day. She suffered from "spinal trouble" and could contribute only fifteen dollars per month to her support. The home expected all its "inmates" (that is what they were called) to pay thirty-five dollars. Her application was denied because she was only fifty-four years old, six years younger than the minimum age requirement of sixty.

Emily Arnold, blind, destitute, and without family, scrawled a note asking whether it might not be possible for her to come to Anderson and spend her last days peacefully among the saints there. Martha Amundson moved into the St. Paul Park home from Clinton, Wisconsin on Christmas Eve, 1908. On the line of her application where the name(s) were to appear of those to be notified of her death she wrote "nobody." Sarah Axtell of Dearborn, Michigan, closed one of her letters to the Anderson home by writing, "P.S., I need your prayers."

People at the Gospel Trumpet Company heard Mrs. Axtell's request for prayer. The heartache in the applicants' letters is matched by an equally impressive note of compassion in the replies of the old people's home managers. They always answered those sad letters, and they always promised their prayers. Their frustration at their inability to help everyone leaps out of their letters denying applicants admission. D. W. Patterson, General Manager of the Gospel Trumpet Company, closed one such letter with the prayer: "May the Lord speed the time when we will be able to give all the old people who are in need of a home the opportunity of coming here."

Given the aspirations of Patterson and the number of "charity cases" admitted to the homes, one may safely conclude that the old people's homes were not considered

Old People's Home

The Old People's Home at Anderson. Built in 1907, the building stood on Fifth Street, east of the Gospel Trumpet Company. Anderson College eventually used the building for a men's dormitory. For a few years college men occupied one part of the building, while remaining aged residents of the home lived in another section.

income-producing properties. They were a ministry of a movement that understood itself, like the earliest Christians, to be charged specifically with the care of the widowed (Acts 6:1) and the recognition of their importance (Acts 9:41). The old people's homes expressed the movement's willingness to extend itself for the benefit of some who could not help themselves.

Our situation has changed dramatically since 1925. Social Security does not benefit all as fully as they need, but it is a vast improvement over the state of affairs in 1925. Greater financial security and better health care mean that a decreasing percentage of persons over the age of sixty-five must live in nursing homes. So it *may* be that our changed social setting does not require of us what it demanded of our predecessors in the Church of God movement. But the gospel still makes requirements of us. Because we have experienced the new birth, we may now live a new life. For whom, for what causes will we extend our resources and ourselves? For what ministry will we pray that God might hasten the day when we might do all that we envision?

THE EVILS OF TIGHT-LACING

Clothing and Christianity seem to have some attributes in common, at least on the surface. The sixteenth century Florentine monk Savonarola organized more than one "Sacrifice of Vanities" in which, among other items, his audiences consigned to the flames their extravagant clothes. More than a thousand years earlier Tertullian wrote an essay in which he attacked the sartorial excesses of Carthaginian Christians. Leafing through the pages of the *Gospel Trumpet,* one will find enough evidence to conclude that we, too, have drawn close connections between faith's vitality and the clothing one wears. Odd, isn't it?

W. J. Henry described the "Evil Effects of Tightlacing" in an 1898 issue of the *Trumpet.* A "tightlaced" woman, in this case, had cinched her bodice down to a fashionable daintiness. Henry did not moralize about corsets. He objected to them "from a physiological standpoint." Tight-lacing was evil because the practice destroyed women's health. Other objections to corsets doubtlessly existed, but Henry was motivated by his concerns about women's physical well-being.

Another kind of concern about clothing focused on a person's prior attitudes and commitments. Another 1898 article "On Dress" flatly doubted that the Christian virtue of humility could coexist with a large wardrobe. Even if that were possible, the article continued, money spent on clothing would not be available for good works: "every shilling which you needlessly spend on your own apparel is in effect stolen from the poor. For what end do you want these ornaments? To please God? No! but to please your own fancy or to gain the admiration and applause of those who are no wiser than yourself." Strong words. Who of us considers a clothing purchase to be a matter of moral consequence?

Ten years later Opal F. Brookover published an article "On Dress." She also targeted the morality of clothing, but now the matter had nothing to do with how dollars not used for clothes might otherwise be spent. Clothing, for Brookover, was a sign by which one could discern saint from worldling. A plain skirt was holier than a pleated one. But saintly women must be certain that they wore "really plain" skirts. Simply because a skirt lacked pleats was no evidence that it was *really* plain. Some pleatless skirts had "nine, some eleven, others thirteen, and still others fifteen gores."

Opal Brookover doubtless would never have worn a corset. But she may have fallen victim to another of the evils of tight-lacing. Now we are speaking of the tight-laced as "stubbornly or rigidly self-contained," "notably and excessively strict in manners, morals or opinion." Opal Brookover, concerned about the number of gores in a really plain skirt, was tight-laced—whether or not she wore a corset.

Among his list of the evils of (corset) tight-lacing, W. J. Henry included its negative effects on facial expression: pallid skin-tone, staring eyes, pinched features, not the slightest hint of a smile. Such faces are recorded in countless photographs in the files of the Archives of the Church of God. Those expressions do not grace only the faces of corseted women, however. Either many men in the early movement wore corsets or the sour faces Henry described could be produced by other stimuli. Maybe the people in those photographs suffered from some of the evils of Opal Brookover's form of tight-lacing. Perhaps other kinds of tight-lacing produced the same symptoms as the ones in W. J. Henry's list. Corsets are not the only producers of tight-laced people.

Why spill so much ink over something as insignificant as clothing? Perhaps our choices about clothing, as expressions of our character and our aspirations of the kind of people we hope to be, are not morally insignificant. That insight of our foremothers and forefathers is worth remembering. But we also must remember that clothing is in itself no badge of holiness. Jesus said that what enters our mouths is not as problematic as what exits them. May not the same lesson be drawn about other matters? What we wear may be a matter of our moral concern without stooping to narrow moralizing.

IS ANY SICK AMONG YOU?

Fifty to seventy-five years ago, leading ministers in the movement often devoted their preaching and teaching to specific theological topics. The movement regarded F. G. Smith as an expert in the area of biblical prophecy. H. M. Riggle was widely known as a specialist on the doctrine of the kingdom of God. When discussions turned to the topic of divine healing, the name of E. E. Byrum was sure to be mentioned.

Enoch Byrum grew up on a farm in Randolph County, Indiana. Manhood came to him sooner than most boys. His father died when Enoch was fifteen, and care of the family farm fell upon his shoulders. While working the farm Enoch received a call to missionary service. But the circumstances of his life were such that he could see no way to answer the call unless the care of his family could be secured; responsi-

E. E. Byrum

E. E. Byrum (1861-1942) and his third wife, Lucena (standing, center) praying for a saint during the divine healing service at Anderson Camp Meeting. Byrum, second editor of the *Gospel Trumpet*, felt himself called and gifted for a ministry of healing. Several of his numerous books and articles deal with the subject of divine healing. While editor, Byrum added a "Divine Healing" feature to the back page of the *Gospel Trumpet*.

bility ran deep in the young man's character. When a way opened up, he sold his share of the farm to an older brother and left for Otterbein College.

While home from school, Enoch heard D. S. Warner's evangelistic company in a meeting. Their message intrigued him. In 1887, after attending a few more meetings in the area, Byrum, along with his friend John Mayne, visited the Bangor, Michigan camp meeting. The most amazing event took place while Enoch attended services there.

Warner owned the Gospel Trumpet Company in partnership with J. C. Fisher. But that partnership broke up in the summer of 1887 when Fisher sued for a divorce from his wife in order to marry another woman. Warner refused to publish a single issue of the paper as a partner in such an unequal yoking. The company had to find someone with enough money to buy out Fisher's interest—and fast. It just so happened that a young man then at the camp meeting had nine-hundred dollars in an Indiana bank account. When Enoch departed the Bangor grounds, he left as the publisher and business manager of the Trumpet Company. He had never put two hours back to back in a printing office, and his managerial experience was limited to that of a small-time farmer. But Byrum possessed the will and character for the work to which he had been called.

When Warner died in 1895, Byrum succeeded to the editor's chair, a position he held until 1916. During those years, under Byrum's influence, the *Gospel Trumpet* and the company's books heavily emphasized the doctrine of divine healing.

Byrum liked to refer to Jesus as the "Great Physician." In fact one of his books carried that title. But Byrum interpreted "physician" as broadly as possible. He believed that Jesus healed sin-sick souls as well as afflicted bodies. So when he quoted the question in James 5:14, Enoch had in mind anyone who suffered any kind of illness.

The reason Byrum could apply this text so inclusively rests in the Church of God's early understanding of God's work in the atoning activity of Jesus. They used to say that there was "healing in the Atonement." By this they meant that Jesus' death on the cross covered all the disastrous consequences of the sin in the garden of Eden. Adam and Eve's sin had introduced spiritual death, physical death, and *sickness* into a world that previously had known nothing of those mortal enemies of humans. As the perfect sacrifice, reasoned early Church of God writers, Jesus must remedy all those evils let loose in the world. So there is healing in the Atonement. But this healing comes not only to bodies; it also restores souls to health.

Byrum interpreted the doctrine of salvation as the restoration of health or wholeness. That is an idea worth remembering. To be saved also means to be rescued, but, appropriately, and especially in Byrum's work, to be saved means to be made whole. The life of Jesus wonderfully brings the healing of our despair, our alienation, our sense of unrooted aloneness. It even overcomes the downward spiral of self-deception that is the special disease of tender souls. There is then a healing wholeness, a *shalom*, in the Atonement.

THE PRESENCE FOR WHICH SOULS THIRST

One cannot read early issues of the *Gospel Trumpet* without noticing the letters printed in the paper. Sometimes they carried testimonies of salvation, sometimes simply exclamations of praise for what the Lord had done in someone's life. Some letters requested prayers for healing. Often they expressed their writers' simple gratitude that another copy of the *Trumpet* had arrived in the mail.

In the movement's early days the saints often found themselves widely scattered. This isolation made Christian fellowship hard to come by. Thus the welcomed arrival of the *Trumpet*—it helped bind scattered saints into a movement. But times of sickness intensified the saints' separateness.

E. E. Byrum taught the Church of God movement the most literal reading of James 5:14-15. When the sick sought divine healing, they were to be anointed with olive oil in the midst of elders who had been called to gather round, lay hands upon the afflicted brother or sister, and pray the prayer of faith. But what of the saint for whom no elders could be found to extend their hands in fellowship and faith?

Byrum discovered a way to overcome the isolation of afflicted saints. Based on Acts 19:12, Byrum mailed anyone who so requested a small handkerchief anointed with oil. He and other workers would pray over the cloth and send it to the isolated saint. When received, the cloth was to be placed on the afflicted part of the body and the prayer of faith repeated—just as if in the presence of gathered elders.

I must confess to having been troubled by the knowledge of this practice. It seems to enter that murky area between religion and magic, making talismen of oil-stained handkerchiefs. Why not simply and honestly assure the lonely petitioner of sympathetic prayer support? Because something must be said for the kind of presence we know only through touching.

We in the Church of God movement have substituted the word *ordinance* for "sacrament." Space does not permit a rehearsal of that argument here. But one aspect of the word sacrament touches the practice of Byrum's anointed handkerchiefs and may yield some insight to us. Originally, the Latin *sacramentum* meant a pledge, commonly a soldier's pledge of loyalty. The sending of an anointed handkerchief was a sacrament in this original sense. Byrum and others pledged their faithful presence through this tactile sign. They promised one of the church's most important tasks in this world— to be present in the lives of those who are afflicted and oppressed, to see to it that they never, ever suffer alone.

One of the soul's mysterious capacities is that of being able to be touched. From touches we sometimes recoil in fear; other times we receive the touch extended by loving hands. Therein lies the importance of E. E. Byrum's anointed hankies. Far from magical charms, they offered the touch of "presence" for which our souls thirst and never more than when we are sick and alone.

Theological Ethics, Politics and History

few miles west of the camp ground.

In 1903 the Church of God movement's theology of healing could not explain very satisfactorily the kind of calamity that struck Nora and Clarence Hunter. By then sickness had come to be regarded as the effect of one of four causes: (a) Satan, who wanted to afflict the soul of the one he made physically sick; (b) God, who wanted to chastise a sinner back to moral health; (c) sin, which led to its own disastrous consequences; or (d) the "sickness-unto-death," meaning that the afflicted person had come to that time appointed for each of us to die. But none of these explanations adequately accounted for the illness and deaths of two innocent babies.

The same year that Nora and Clarence were married a young man named Charles Wesley Naylor offered his services to the Gospel Trumpet Company. They accepted him and put him to work in the subscriptions department. Before long he was writing books and poetry set to music for the hymnals and songbooks published by the company. His many songs include "The Church's Jubilee," "Once Again We Come," "More Like Christ," "I Am the Lord's," and the beautiful "Spirit Holy."

Trumpet workers, even poets, labored at a variety of manual tasks when sweat and elbow grease were required. Naylor also did his share of heavy work. But an accident occurred while he worked setting up a large meeting tent, and Naylor sustained severe internal injuries. He never recovered and eventually was left bedfast and in unrelieved pain. God could not be blamed for the accident, but why wasn't Naylor healed? More than one person who knew of the case asked that question. Despite the fact that some came to Naylor's bedside to be anointed for healing by him, slanderous stories circulated about the poet's "hidden sin."

Naylor, too, wondered why God did not restore him to full physical health. A line from the song he wrote with Clarence Hunter, "God's way is best, I will not murmur," expresses the answer Naylor got to his question. From his pen also comes a sentence that enlarged our theology of healing, if only we will hear it: "Pain is God's chisel, with which he carves his image in the heart."

In our time and place, when we look for ways to avoid suffering at all cost, Naylor's words seem callous and only cold comfort. He did not say that we should seek pain, but when suffering visits us, we may also find God at work bringing to perfection a work already begun. Naylor's poetry, his books, and his life enable us to speak a word of consolation to others who have suffered in ways like Nora and Clarence Hunter—those who have lost a child in a senseless accident, those who have lost a spouse in a dreadful fight with cancer, those who see the morning's happiness evaporate in swift unimaginable loss. Charles Naylor gave words to the mystery that embraces suffering people of faith. He knew for them, and for us, that especially in those places, the God of heartache is at work, chiseling out the divine image with a wholeness, a *shalom*, a peace that passes all understanding.

THE GREAT NECKTIE CONTROVERSY

In the last years of the last decade of the nineteenth century, a group of ministers led by W. A. Haynes, W. J. Henry, E. G. Masters and others revised their teaching on sanctification. Like other holiness movement groups of that time, the Church of God movement had interpreted sanctification according to one side of John Wesley's thought, that popularized by Adam Clarke of commentary fame. In essence, this view said that God's grace operated twice in a person's life, initially at justification and subsequently at sanctification. The first work God does *for* us; the second is done *in* us.

One group deviated from this generally held doctrine and began teaching an interpretation in which sanctification was thought to take place at the same moment that persons were justified. Because these teachings were associated with Nicholas Zinzendorf, Wesley's sometime friend and theological opponent, the novel teaching soon acquired the label "Zinzendorfism." Because a part of Zinzendorf's teaching included the idea of "imputed" (but not real) sanctification, Zinzendorfism also became known by its opponents as the "anti-cleansing heresy."

The word *heresy* marks the serious nature of the controversy. More than theological subtleties were at stake; schism, the sin against unity, was in the air. In the aftermath of the tension-filled Moundsville Camp Meeting of 1899 a serious rupture indeed occurred. Some of the best preachers left the movement, but they never coalesced into a group. Some joined denominational churches or other groups such as the Disciples of Christ. Others found their way back into the fellowship of the Church of God movement. The movement's understanding of sanctification was not resolved, however, with the end of the anti-cleansing conflict.

In 1903 C. E. Orr published *Christian Conduct*. This little book focused the movement's attention on its practical expression of the doctrine of sanctification. Ever since Warner's early days as a holiness preacher, the outward form of the sanctified life had been the subject of numerous Church of God sermons. Orr's book put the matter in the spotlight. The recent debate over Zinzendorfism only served to narrow the beam of that light. Together, Orr's book and the earlier debate brought the question of appropriate Christian behavior to an incendiary point.

For men the necktie became the great watershed of practical sanctification. Wearing one signaled worldliness; forsaking the tie demonstrated holiness. It scarcely seems possible that such an innocent article of clothing threatened to divide a movement called to witness to Christian unity. The controversy seems ironically humorous, but the irony is almost too painful to endure. When Christians either threaten or, worse, act out self-division, they further rend Christ's seamless robe, and that scarcely seems a laughing matter. Whether ironic or tragic, C. E. Orr and many others broke fellowship with Christians who would not join in a resolution against wearing "the tie."

By 1915 Orr had repented his actions and rejoined the

movement. But the seeds of what he and others had sown continued to reap a bitter harvest. So it is when we sin against love. But does not God's love stand even against our sins against love? Maybe even in this all-too-serious episode that is farcical, but for its sad consequences, there remains yet a hint of divine humor. Perhaps Robert Louis Stevenson was right when he wrote, "For the life of man upon this world of ours is a funny business. They talk of the angels weeping, but I think they must more often be holding their sides, as they look on" (Stevenson 1974:427).

HANDSHAKE RELIGION

In 1895 two Church of God evangelists traveled to Federalsburg, Maryland. Nora Hunter and Lena Shoffner held forth in revival meetings there for six weeks. They sang and prayed; they exhorted mightily. But no spiritual harvest resulted from their labors. So one night they announced that if nobody was saved in the next meeting that service would conclude the revival. The next service arrived, and at its conclusion a man rose to give his heart to the Lord. Others followed and, in Hazel Neal's words, "A congregation was born overnight" (Neal 17).

Shoffner had been converted through the Warner evangelistic company's work in Missouri only five years earlier. Lena became one of the first members of the Carthage congregation. But her flaming spirit could not be confined to southwest Missouri. Her passion for the gospel eventually carried her on an evangelistic tour of England, concentrating particularly on the cities of London and Liverpool.

In 1903 Shoffner opened a revival in Oklahoma City. The nature of her gospel labor changed here, for she remained for the next eight years as the first regular Church of God pastor in that town. She also married Ed Mattheson. Together they served the church as Oklahoma pastors and evangelists until Lena's death at age sixty-eight in 1937.

Like many other Church of God preachers and evangelists, Lena Shoffner's spirit was forged in the fires of revivalism.

Walking with God: The Church and Morality

among the more interesting and troubling aspects of American political life in the last decade of the twentieth century is the intensity and the fruitlessness of our moral debate. Television news programs regularly broadcast film of either abortion opponents or advocates marching in protest or support of government policies implemented since the Roe v. Wade decision. Both protesters and supporters of capital punishment can usually be found outside the walls of a prison on the eve of a condemned prisoner's execution. Magazine articles discuss the possibilities and fears associated with our society's growing acceptance of euthanasia. These are but a few examples of the moral debates that have become standard elements of modern American life.

That these debates are both intense and fruitless of any enduring solution can be traced, in large measure, to the absence of any coherent moral tradition in our society. No person has identified this absence or drawn out its implications with greater insight than the philosopher Alasdair MacIntyre. In one of the most significant books of the

1980s, *After Virtue*, MacIntyre attributes American culture's inability to reach conclusions in our moral debates to a lost moral consensus. We no longer speak a common moral language, as it were. Instead, our moral debates employ disconnected concepts that are drawn from different and often conflicting moral traditions.

For example, most of us agree that humans possess the right to determine what happens to their own bodies. That we sign releases in hospitals by which we grant physicians permission to treat our bodies illustrates our general acceptance of this moral principle. It has some moral, and in this case legal, force. Of course, many of those who advocate the general availability of abortion base their argument in this position. They are often opposed by those who would deny abortion to all on the grounds that "all life is sacred." That, too, is a valid moral principle. Now we have two moral principles, both of which seem valid, being employed against each other. We are fighting apples with oranges, so to speak, because these two principles rise out of different moral systems. When we abstract principles from their larger moral systems our moral debate becomes incoherent. Then we resort to the only tactic we think will clarify the thought of those who do not understand us: we talk louder and louder, until we are shouting.

Can any light be shed on this otherwise very dark picture? MacIntyre suggests that the only viable strategy in a morally diverse culture like ours is the reestablishment of communities on the basis of identifiable moral traditions. While large pluralistic societies may no longer be capable of recovering their moral coherence, that need not be the case for smaller communities that may still draw upon their moral traditions, i.e., their story or narrative.

The church is one such community that possesses at least the capacity for the recovery of its moral coherence through the various acts of remembrance that form its life together. Critics of the church like Stanley Hauerwas and William Willimon believe that the church may yet recover its moral coherence. This recovery will not be easy or without cost. It will require basic changes in our fundamental ways of viewing and understanding the church and morality.

MacIntyre's analysis and arguments are more than plausible; they are convincing. They lead to the realization that any religious tradition, any church group or denomination, would do well to understand its moral tradition and offer some account of how ethics ought to be understood and enacted. In light of that realization, this essay rather ambitiously intends to speak to several important questions: (1) How has the Church of God movement understood Christian ethics? What have been our approaches to the important issues of moral philosophy? What have our leading theologians said about Christian ethics? (2) What have we thought about the Bible as a moral authority? (3) How, in the Church of God movement, can we connect the theological idea of sanctification with Christian ethics? and (4) What then would be a viable proposal for the future concerning the Church of God and its approach to Christian ethics?

Needless to say, these are large questions, and they might very well comprise a monograph or even a book. But my purpose here is to introduce these questions, rather than write a detailed exposition of any one or all of them. This essay intends to introduce readers to the way we in the Church of God movement have thought about and practiced Christian ethics. As such it is an exercise in remembering. At the very least, the church's act of remembering is, or ought to be, a moral and political art. As G. K. Chesterton said, remembering one's tradition is the way we invite our forefathers and foremothers to cast a vote about the kind of people we believe God is calling us to be.

I

To reconstruct the Church of God movement's ethical practice from the pages of books in theology and ethics is a hazardous strategy. A researcher who quotes from any Church of God book is necessarily citing the views of one person. The question remains concerning how representative those books were, and are, of wider opinion or belief in the movement. Not infrequently some gap exists between the formal presentations of theological and moral publications and the practices of the movement.

A good example of this disparity can be seen in the movement's early published positions on pacifism and its actual practice. If one only read the printed statements of early Church of God leaders, he or she quickly would conclude that the Church of God movement opposed war and that, therefore, its men entered the military only as noncombatants if they entered it at all. All the public statements agreed that since human life is sacred, to kill a human being is a sin of the gravest consequence.

Anyone who carefully reads the *Gospel Trumpet* during the years 1914-1918, however, will discover a practice somewhat at odds with public statements of pacifism (Strege 1991). Despite printed opposition to war and killing, it is apparent that several men from the Church of God entered military service during World War I. I mention this not to begin a debate on pacifism, but to illustrate the distance that sometimes occurs between the church's formal theological statements and the church's practice. This distance is a problem for people who wish to describe the church's historical position on moral or theological matters. Does the researcher write about what has been written or what has been practiced? Because written statements and practice are not unrelated, ultimately we must take account of both in any account of ethics in the Church of God. That is the method I will try to follow here, beginning with some published theological and philosophical works that deal with the subject of Christian ethics.

Church of God writers have devoted comparatively little attention to the formal subject of Christian ethics. This inattention seems odd because the Church of God movement has devoted a considerable amount of theological attention to the doctrine of sanctification, which seems the natural starting point for a discussion of ethics. We have published numerous books on what might be called the Christian life and subjects thereof, however.[1] We have been quite concerned about the behavior and character of the new man or woman in Christ, even if we have not written many formal theories of ethics. We have apparently thought of Christian ethics as the character of the Christian even though we have not developed that conception in extended fashion. That conclusion already says something extremely significant about our conception of Christian ethics and the possibilities for developing and clarifying that thought.

Among formal works that deal with theories of ethics, the largest and most systematic presentation published by a Church of God writer is Warner Monroe's *An Introduction to Christian Ethics* (1947). That this book is so infrequently cited is curious considering the scope and detail of its argument. Monroe both described general theories of ethics and offered his own approach to Christian ethics. He thought that the "morally earnest person" asks the ethical question in this form: "What choices in life are right?" Monroe also believed "in the possibility of discovering unconditional or categorical laws of right being, which apply not to this or that chosen type of life or activity, but to all human life whatsoever. Furthermore, he (the morally serious person) is led to seek for a single principle whereby certain acts or purposes, or even rules of living, are described as right" (14).

Monroe was heavily influenced by the philosophy of Immanuel Kant. This influence may be seen in the quotation cited above as well as in Monroe's description of virtue as the "disposition to do right" and his belief that "we can arrive at a knowledge of virtue by reconsidering the nature of right" (212-13). Kant thought about ethics within a framework of theories that often are described as nonconsequentialist. In this approach to ethics what counts as most important are the rules or principles that direct our moral choice. Ethics becomes a matter of right decision, and the foundational principles provide the knowledge necessary to choose rightly. If the principle is, "Do not tell a lie" then we should never, under any circumstances, tell a lie—regardless of the consequences. The complete disregard of the consequences in obedience to the principle gives this approach to ethics its name—nonconsequentialism.[2]

Religious versions of nonconsequentialism often are termed "divine command" ethics. The moral life is conceived as the making of right choices, and choosing rightly is simply a matter of obeying the commandments of God. Great emphasis is laid on the Christian's obligation to do his or her moral duty, which is obedience. Although Monroe's book states moral theory and issues more formally than is normally the case among Church of God clergy and lay persons, I think that they would be sympathetic toward his divine command approach. Church of God preaching has often been motivated by a powerful sense of Christian duty.

A Scandinavian-American immigrant member of the Church of God expressed this sense when she wrote, "Man's duty is to do the Lord's will and this is found laid down in his Word. Indeed the more often we read and examine the inspired Scriptures the better we will understand God's will and our duty. Through doing our duty we please God" (Simonsen 1906:4). To live a moral life, in this view, is to live a life pleasing to God, and we please God by doing our duty, i.e., obeying God's will, regardless of the consequences. Any number of Bible verses can be cited in support of the idea of Christian obligation or duty. Virtually any verse written in the imperative mode can be employed to reinforce divine command ethics.

Although the idea of ethics as duty is an important theme in the popular piety of the Church of God, it is only one theme within a more comprehensive notion. We might term that larger notion the idea of ethics as "walking with God." Church of God people have linked their moral aspirations with their piety, for the aspiration of the latter was to live continuously in the Lord's presence or, as they put it, "walk with God." While it was not the result of a studied understanding of the Old Testament, the Church of God's notion of walking with God has affinities with the Hebrew ideal of walking in the way of Yahweh.

Historically, the Church of God regarded the goal of

human existence as the soul's perfect walk through life in intimate relationship with God. Walking with God meant walking in the footsteps of Christ. Such devotion was impossible except for those "who have seen Jesus in the heart and have crucified the flesh with its lusts and desires" (*Den Evangeliske Basun* May 15 1904:4). Undergoing the crucifixion of the flesh signified the believer's possession of the mind of Christ. Once the individual comes to own "Christ's humble mind," he or she will be able to conquer all of life's difficulties, and the soul will be filled with joy.

Divine guidance was available to believers for the difficult and dangerous journey through the world. Four resources often were mentioned as guides for the people of God in their walk with God: (1) the Scriptures, (2) inner impressions from the Holy Spirit, (3) "sanctified judgment," and (4) circumstance. Church of God writers did not invest these resources with magical qualities. Neither did people in the movement claim to have visions or supernatural revelations. Instead they adopted a rather common sense approach to the ability to discern the Lord's leading. The person who possessed the mind of Christ should be able to discern God's will with no greater difficulty than an apple tree produces apples. Early saints also believed that one always had recourse to the Bible as the final arbiter of the trustworthiness of impressions that seem to have their source in God; godly impressions conformed to Scripture. As one early saint put the matter, "Preserve yourself in Jesus and his word, and you will be led in the right way" (Gahmann 1904:6).

Curiously absent from the list of resources that enable the saints to walk with God is the church. That the Church of God movement has thought, written, preached, and sung so much about the church only adds to a curiosity that prompts one to ask: Why did the Church of God movement leave unconnected its ideas about the church and walking with God? One possible answer to that question is that the movement has thought of the church as the consequence of the salvation of individual souls. In such a view the church is the aggregate of all the saved on earth rather than an authoritative resource for the shaping of the Christian life. Correlative to this is the early leaders' deep suspicion of organized religion. Several of them had experienced what they felt to be the heavy hand of church authority. They insisted that the true church would be absent of the kind of authority they commonly called "ecclesiasticism." But the early leaders' great desire to escape authoritarian church structures may have obscured their vision of the church's role in contributing to the moral development of the individual members.[3] Ironically, therefore, the Church of God movement's theology of the church may severely limit the church's influence on the moral development of its individual members.

Recent works in Christian ethics have begun restating the importance of the community, the people of God, for ethics. In different approaches both James McLendon and William Willimon intimately connect the church with the moral life of Christians.[4] Much may be said for this connection, but it only makes sense in a conception of Christian ethics that thinks less of the obedient response of individuals to the will of God and more of walking with God toward the goal of the maturing of Christian character, i.e., the moral development of men and women unto the measure of the stature of the fullness of Christ.

Another answer to the question, "Why hasn't the church of God seen the connection between church and ethics?" lies in the movement's revivalism. There is no mystery about the reason why *revival* is such a beloved word in the Church of God. The movement came into existence at a time when the revival was approaching the zenith of its popularity and influence as a technique of mass evangelism. Holding a revival was to the nineteenth-century American church what the church growth movement threatens to become in the late twentieth. Its great popularity stamped its impress on Church of God expectations about worship and preaching.

Revivalism's great success in the latter half of the nineteenth century shaped the conceptions of church and ministry in new religious movements like the Church of God. Under the influence of revivalism, the minister's primary role came to be that of evangelist, and the evangelistic style of preaching became normative in the Church of God and much of American Protestantism (cf. Mead 1985). Worship took on the air of the revival meeting. Such an ethos emphasizes the instantaneous shift from sin to grace, from worldliness to godliness. In its concern to rescue the unsaved, revivalism created a conception of church and Christian life that tends to overlook the gradual process of moral development that occurs within a nurturing community. Divine command theories of ethics, on the other hand, were quite adaptable to the revivalistic milieu. It is thus understandable why a revivalistic tradition like the Church of God has generally thought of ethics as divine command and emphasized moral categories like obedience and duty to the right.

II

One might describe the Church of God movement as an extended conversation about the implications of the gospel story for Christian discipleship and the church. We have been deeply concerned about the meaning of Scripture for our lives as followers of Jesus and as the body of Christ. Our theologians have probed the questions and issues related to our search for biblical holiness and the unity of all Christians.

Salvation inaugurates the believer's pilgrimage toward holiness and unity. But we have inherited from the Wesleyan theological tradition a comprehensive understanding of salvation. In this understanding, salvation is the result of God's gracious action both for us and in us. God justifies us, which means that our relationship with God has been changed. But then God also regenerates us, which means that the new creature in Christ has been born in us. In Wesleyan terms, this rebirth is the beginning of growth until the moment when we may be said to be entirely sanctified. This experience of sanctification then introduces the believer to the life of holiness. In classical Wesleyan theology, conversion and sanctification together comprise the salvation of the human being.

A. F. Gray, founding president of Warner Pacific College and professor of systematic theology there, described the Christian life in developmentalist terms. God's work of salvation introduced the believer to the Holy Spirit, as Gray put it. "The presence of the Spirit makes one holy, but he will grow in holiness in the development of a more holy character. The Christian life is a growth in grace as well as knowledge" (1946:86-87). Gray did not think that a person could grow into sanctification; that required God's grace. But he did think that "the Spirit-filled life is one of constant increase in power and continued improvement" (86-87).

C. E. Brown, fourth editor of the *Gospel Trumpet*, was a prolific writer. Of the more than a dozen books that he wrote, *The Meaning of Sanctification* intensively examined all the dimensions of life in the Spirit. Like Gray and R. R. Byrum (1925:463), Brown refused to endorse the idea of a sanctification that could be achieved through human effort (1945:156-157). But Brown also believed that new Christians will engage in the "slow and sometimes tedious task of acquiring spiritual skill in the realm of Christian life where [they] will labor" (175).

Gilbert Stafford, current speaker on the Christian Brotherhood Hour and a professor of systematic theology, studied the doctrine of salvation as presented by seven Church of God theological writers as part of his doctoral study at Boston University. Stafford's own theological work bears marks of their influence upon him. He describes salvation as a "way of life" into which we are introduced by God's grace (1979:v). Salvation is more than God's declaration of the believer's righteousness. Stafford's point here, I take it, is to rebut Reformation theology's idea of a forensic justification. So he says that salvation is a "lifelong involvement of faith instead of a mere once-in-a-while statement of faith" (v).

We might use the metaphor of the pilgrimage to describe the life of discipleship, a figure of speech that Stafford himself employs. The life of salvation is a journey from sin and hopelessness to the hope-filled fullness of the life of Christ. Indeed, "there is no scriptural evidence whatsoever that indicates that the will of God is anything less than that we grow up into the fullness of Christ" (34-35).

Stafford also believes that the experience of salvation always is communal. "The *personal* life of faith is seen as part of the *communal* life of faith. . . . New Testament Christianity is communal Christianity. To be saved is to be added to the community of restored relationships" (100). Here, in this expressly stated connection between salvation and the church, Stafford echoes a point made countless times by Church of God preachers and writers. "The church is the organism through which [God] works . . . ," the invisible expression of the new race, the organ of a redeemed humanity. . . . The church is the community of God. It is a colony of heaven" (Martin 1942:179-183, *passim*).

I have summarized salient points from the work of several respected and representative theologians of the Church of God to make the point that within our conception of the life of salvation are embedded several themes that lend themselves to a particular approach to theological ethics. Given the affinity of our theological tradition with this particular ethical framework, it would seem only to make sense that we understand it and explore the possibilities of its application to the movement's life and thought. The themes to which I am referring are (a) that the life of salvation requires the presence of the church, (b) that the life of salvation is a way of life and a pilgrimage, and (c) that the goal of this journey is to grow up to the fullness of Christ, to display a holy character. I wish to suggest that these points do not translate well into either consequentialist or nonconsequentialist moral theories. Rather, such points are far more congenial to an approach that can be called character or virtue ethics.

Edmund Pincoffs convincingly argues that a problem with much of contemporary moral philosophy is that it neglects the question of the character of the agent (1986:13-36). All too frequently our energy is directed at efforts to construct rules or extract from "the situation" principles that will either command or guide the moral deliberations of the person about to act. Such efforts disregard the character of the person who must decide to act. What is important in modern moral philosophy is the construction of a calculus to govern our moral reflection. Pincoffs argues that the neglect of the moral agent's character is precisely the problem of modern moral philosophy. Our moral reflection must begin instead, he contends, with the question, "What kind of person is this who is about to act? What is his or her character?" For the character of the agent exerts a determinative influence on the situation.

Students in my ethics courses have become accustomed to hearing me make the Hauerwasian observation that our most important moral commitments are made in connection with the statement "I had no choice." This statement means that a situation that might be morally ambiguous for someone else is not necessarily problematic for everyone. A person possessed of a different character, in the same situation, might have no question about his or her course of action.[5] Moreover, when someone explains an action (or a nonaction) by the phrase "I had no choice" we ought to pay close attention, for we are about to be given the opportunity to peer into that person's very character.

This observation confirms the determinative influence that character exerts on the situation. Because of the kind of persons we are, the situation may not require us to make a decision at all. Our character will determine our perspective on the situation in ways that may preclude the need for a decision. Or our character may cause us to see the situation as one that presents us with only one option. If character has this kind of determinative influence, then we clearly must acquire at least an elementary knowledge of character ethics.

III

Alasdair MacIntyre argues for the recovery of character ethics, which he refers to as the "classical" approach. Those who wish to explore this rich and provocative argument in detail should refer to *After Virtue.* Here I wish only to outline his description of classical systems of ethics. The framework of this system can be most stimulating for moral reflection in the Church of God movement.

Classical systems of ethics, whether heroic, Aristotelian, or New Testament, include four major components: an idea of the human self as oriented to some *telos*, traditions, or narratives that sustain the unity of that self, communities that sustain those narratives/traditions and in which the self is nourished and grows to maturity, and a table of virtues that are both means and expressions of the life well-lived.

(a) the self in relation to a *telos*

Here we are thinking generally of human life as ordered to a given end. Our lives do not begin with the irreducible individual, but with a whole web of relationships out of which our selfhood grows. In classical moral systems the absence of this web renders a person a nonentity or a stranger or outcast at best. "To know oneself as such a social person is, however, not to occupy a static and fixed position. It is to find oneself placed at a certain point on a journey with set goals; to move through life is to make progress—or to fail to make progress—toward a given end" (1984:34). One thinks in this connection of Paul's aspiration to press on to the mark of the high calling of Christ Jesus and that in using *hamartia* the New Testament saw that sin was the failure to treat life as this kind of moral project. In classical moral systems, the self is not free to develop into whatever you will. Self-realization is an impossible conception in moral systems with a view of human life (and self) as ordered to a given end. Instead the self must learn from an authoritative moral tradition what the end or *telos* of human life might be.

(b) a unified self sustained by narrative/tradition

Only in one small sense is it true that narratives are

rendered by bards and storytellers. In point of fact there is, as Stephen Crites has observed, a narrative quality to human experience, and it is that ability to recount a narrative that gives coherence and continuity to our selfhood (1971:291-311). "Narrative form is neither disguise nor decoration" (MacIntyre 211):

> Humans are in their actions and practices, as well as their fictions, essentially storytelling creatures. [They] are not essentially, but become through their histories, tellers of stories that aspire to truth . . . I can only answer the question 'What am I to do?' if I can answer the prior question 'of what story or stories do I find myself a part?' We enter human society, that is, with one or more imputed characters—roles into which we have been drafted—and we have to learn what they are in order to be able to understand how others respond to us and how our responses to them are apt to be construed. It is through hearing stories about wicked stepmothers, lost children, good but misguided kings . . . youngest sons who waste their inheritance on riotous living and go into exile to live with the swine, that children learn or mislearn both what a child and what a parent is, what the cast of characters may be in the drama into which they have been born, and what the ways of the world are. Deprive children of stories and you leave them unscripted, anxious stutterers in their actions as in their words (216).

(c) communities that sustain the self and embody a specific narrative

Edmund Pincoffs observed that when the Apostle Paul said *we*, he "spoke from within a community of expectations and ideals: a community within which character was cultivated" (1986:34). Classical systems of ethics understand the self not as "individual" but as defined by and growing to maturity in relationship to a larger community. Paul's metaphor for this is the church as the body of Christ. In such an understanding a man or woman, once cut off from the corporate body, cannot come to fulfillment because the person severed from the body cannot fulfill the function intrinsic to full humanity realized in that corporate life. A hand severed from the body no longer can function as a hand. Thus we are justified in concluding that it no longer is a hand, despite all appearances. That was Plato's theory of the relationship of the free person to the city-state as well as Paul's idea of responsible Christian existence.

(d) a table of virtues that are both means and expressions of the life well-lived

Virtue is a word often misunderstood and misapplied. In our time, virtue has come to mean a "disposition necessary to produce obedience to the rules of morality" (MacIntyre 1984:232). In classical systems of ethics, the virtue (*arete*) of anything was the ability it possessed to perform its function. Courage was virtuous to the soldier because cowardice frustrated his ability to fulfill his *telos*. The absence of courage meant that the soldier could not fulfill his purpose, could not reach his *telos*. Love heads the list of virtues Paul refers to as the harvest of the Spirit in Galatians 5:22 because love enables the Christian man or woman to fulfill his or her *telos*. *Tables of virtues are lists of these qualities essential to the realization of the telos.* In addition to the list in Galatians 5:22-23, one may find tables of Christian virtues in Colossians 3:12-14 and 2 Peter 1:5-7. Being a person of love, joy, peace, long-suffering, and the like means that we display in our lives those qualities that both express and are the means toward the realization of a well-lived life.

This brief description of classical or character ethics should be sufficient to enable us to ask whether it is a conception of ethics congenial to the theological tradition of the Church of God. That question can be answered in the affirmative for several reasons.

In our summary of Church of God theologians I identified

the commonly held theme of the Christian life as a journey-pilgrimage. The goal of this pilgrimage is Christlikeness. Christians believe that Jesus is not only the Savior, but the Second Adam. As such he is the divine restatement of what God intends for humanity to be. To believe thus is to believe that human beings have a *telos* or a goal toward which their moral growth is intended. Thus the commonly held conception of the Christian life as a pilgrimage or journey entails the notion of a *telos* for that life. Clearly this is compatible with the first category in MacIntyre's description of character ethics.

Second, in the Church of God movement, salvation and church have been intricately linked. Salvation is not only personal but communal. Although this connection may have been weakened by our revivalistic individualism, nevertheless the church has been an important factor in our theology of Christian discipleship. I will not dispute the fact that at times the church has oppressively made its expectations of people. But the church has also functioned as a community of expectation in which Christlike character has flourished.

The Church of God movement also has identified tables of virtues. We may be most familiar with them in their negative forms as the prohibition of vices such as gambling, consumption of alcohol, the use of tobacco, and the like. I will concede the point that much of our language here has emphasized the absence of vice rather than the presence of virtues. Nevertheless, where conceptions of vice predominate, we should be able to move to discussions of the virtues. Such discussions have not been entirely absent from our moral reflection and preaching. We have not been negative only in our ideas of virtues and vices.

MacIntyre's description of classical or character ethics includes the idea of narrative. This idea has been expressed in the life of the Church of God movement in at least three ways. Some readers may be taken aback that my first illustration of narrativity in the Church of God is Elsie Egermeier's *Bible Story Book.* But generations of children have first encountered the Bible as in point of fact what it is—the story of God's dealings with the creation and its creatures. It is a story, which we believe to be true, that starts in Genesis and culminates in the Revelation. But, second, in another sense we have understood the story of God's dealings with humankind not to have ended in the Revelation but to be ongoing. This ongoing story is not some new divine disclosure, but the ongoing narrative of God's activity in the world. This confidence in God's continuing narrative in the world has enabled generations of Church of God people to sing, "There's a mighty reformation sweeping o'er the land. God is gathering his people by his mighty hand." Third, the Church of God's sense of God's ongoing activity was not limited to the broad sweep of history. This activity could reach into the individual human heart. Thus the testimony was an especially important form of narrative, for it told the story of God's activity in the human heart and life. The testimony, shared in numberless meetings, is perhaps the fundamental expression of narrative's importance in the life of the Church of God movement.

I hope the force of this comparison will be to suggest that character ethics is a form of ethical reflection highly appropriate to the Church of God movement. Theories of ethics that are focused on obligation or duty too narrowly conceive of ethics as a matter of doing good or right. Before the decision of what to do lies the matter of character, and character, as we have seen, is dependent upon *telos*, community, narrative, and virtues. Because the theological tradition of the Church of God possesses marked affinities with the classical tradition of ethics, we should shift the focus of our reflection on theological ethics from the question "What would God have me do?" to the prior question, "What kind of people is God calling us to be?"

Chapter 5 Notes

1. An impressionistic survey of a cumulative list of Gospel Trumpet Company/Warner Press books that deal with aspects of the Christian life yields the following results: C. E.

Orr 1903; C. W. Naylor 1925; Naylor 1919; Naylor 1922; many others could be cited in addition.

2. The other major family of theories that deal with moral choice is called "consequentialism." Like nonconsequentialists, these people think that morality is first and foremost a matter of right choices. But consequentialists, as their name implies and quite opposite of nonconsequentialists, look to the likely or the desired outcome of the proposed action to determine whether it ought to be chosen. Utilitarianism, where we act to realize the greatest good for the greatest number, is but one example of consequentialist ethics.

3. The Church of God movement illustrates what the American religious historian Nathan O. Hatch has termed, "populist Christianity." Among its characteristics is a hostility to traditional forms of authority like ecclesiastical structures, formal theological training, and the like. Hatch argues that the democratizing forces of the early national period were also at work among religious Americans. In some cases, democratization would seem to meant the virtual inability to conceive of the church as a disciplining community. (Cf. *The Democratization of American Christianity*, 1989).

4. In *Systematic Theology* vol. I: *Ethics*, McLendon argues that in traditions such as the Church of God, one major strand of the rope of Christian ethics is "social," i.e., the strand of the church. William Willimon narrows that focus to the worship of the believing community in his fine book, *The Service of God: How Worship and Ethics are Related* (1983).

5. I must tell here once again the story of my late friend Keith Pulford. Keith and I were high school classmates. He was a split end on the football team and in fine physical condition. The summer between our freshman and sophomore college years he got a job working at a packing plant. He worked at vacation relief, which meant that every other Friday afternoon he learned what he would be doing the next week, for that was when he was trained to replace the worker about to go on vacation.

One hot August Friday, Keith was taken up to the sheep kill, where he discovered that his job for the next two weeks was to be slitting the throats of sheep. As soon as the knife was placed in his hand, Keith handed it back with the words, "I'm sorry, but I can't do that. I have no choice."

Obviously, a football player possesses the strength for the task to which Keith had been assigned. So when he said that he could not kill sheep, he did not mean that he lacked the requisite physical strength. Rather, because of the kind of person he had become, Keith could not kill sheep. His character was such that this was not a situation about which he had to decide. His character had already determined what he would do.

Managers and Sages: The Idea of Authority & the Church of God Movement

6

uthority is one of those elemental ideas that always seems to precede the rest of our thinking whether in matters of theology or polity. Furthermore, recent events underscore the importance of the idea and exercise of authority in the Church of God movement. These events, within and without the movement, have raised questions of authority in the church to the very forefront of our attention. They are also implicit in the deliberations of an ongoing national task force on governance and polity. Clearly the topic of the discussions in which we are about to engage is both timely and important.

When you are the church's historian you are expected to "say something historical," although I'm never quite sure what that means. Saying something historical to Americans is risky, because as a people we have tended to think, like Henry Ford, that "history is bunk." I intend to say something historical, but my references to concrete events and ideas about authority in the Church of God will occur somewhat further down the road. For, while I suspect that most of us think we know what we mean by "authority," in actuality

this is a very complex idea, capable of very different under-
standings with equally diverse implications for the life of the
church. For that reason an examination of the ideas of tradition and authority is important before proceeding to a consideration of the manner in which authority has been exercised in the Church of God movement.

I

Suppose I were to say that in my research for this essay I
had discovered a definitive statement by D. S. Warner on
the nature and application of authority. What then should
be our attitude toward that statement itself? Are Warner's
words "authoritative" and, if so, in what sense? Are they
open to critical scrutiny and reflection? May we deviate
from their prescription in any sense? Suppose further that
Warner's statement was flatly contradicted by his successor,
E. E. Byrum? Would we regard the former's statements as
any more authoritative than those of the latter? Byrum,
F. G. Smith and others succeeded Warner as editor of the
Gospel Trumpet Company, so one might say that they
shared one mantle of authority at different periods of time.
But we could put a sharper edge on the issue and ask
whether the editors' statements are any more authoritative
than those of H. C. Wickersham, a respected early writer in
the movement. If they are, what is it that makes them so?

At this point I want to consider what might be a proper
attitude toward the movement's history and the numerous
publications that document the development of its thought.
A question is already raised about authority insofar as the
church's theology is concerned.[1] Are we bound to think no
further and no differently than those who have already
written or spoken? Is that what we mean by authority in
theology?

Jaroslav Pelikan has provided us with a valuable distinction between two attitudes toward the statements of the
past. The first of these he calls "traditionalism," by which he
means the "dead faith of the living" (1985:65). This attitude

regards all change as bad. It embalms the statements of the past and seals off any possibility of further discussion or change. But the concern of those who take this view is not only negative; they highly prize the continuity of their teaching with the past. Indeed traditionalists make continuity the pearl of great price.

Traditionalism is not, however, the only attitude we may take toward the past, says Pelikan. There remains the possibility of a healthy tradition—"the living faith of the dead." From this perspective we look "through and beyond the statements and judgments of the past, to that living reality of which [they are] an embodiment" (54-55). Religious people of tradition also prize continuity, but they temper it with the recognition that doctrine also develops.

We might illustrate Pelikan's observation by reference to the Church of God's doctrine of divine healing. Clearly this doctrine has undergone considerable development since the days of D. S. Warner, who permitted the saints' use of naturally occurring remedies (herb teas and the like), but refused permission to consult physicians or resort to prescription medicines. Before Warner was cold in his grave, E. E. Byrum moved naturally occurring remedies to the forbidden list; doctrine was thereby modified.

Clearly these teachings changed again since David Gaulke, M.D. practiced medicine as a part of his missionary calling in the 1940s. Today Church of God people regularly consult physicians without a crisis of conscience or faith, and yet we commonly anoint those who are sick or afflicted and pray the prayer of faith for their healing according to James 5:14 as has been our practice since the movement's early days. A traditionalist, attempting to maintain strict continuity with that early doctrinal position, would conclude that both our doctrine and practice had been corrupted. On the other hand, a person of tradition could approve the subsequent developments as extensions of a doctrine with which they were in continuity.

In our better moments we in the Church of God movement have been people of tradition rather than traditionalism. We have honored the work of those who came before 1880 without making an idol of it. Similarly we respect the work of previous authors in the movement without elevating it to the status of a creed. Thus John W. V. Smith said in his last book, "All theological writing in the Church of God . . . is one person's voice" (1985:4). Dr. Smith shared this basic attitude toward the past with F. G. Smith, who wrote these words about the historic creeds of Christianity:

> These documents may express many noble sentiments respecting Christ and his truth, and they may express the fullest knowledge of the truth known in the days when they were written. But knowledge of the truth is progressive, while creeds are stationary. No human document, therefore, can serve as a permanent basis upon which to build our faith (1919:130).

As I say, this has been our attitude toward the past in our better moments; there have been lesser ones. A decade after F. G. Smith published the words quoted immediately above, the General Ministerial Assembly defeated his resolution on standard literature, and thereby reminded him that the attitude toward the past expressed in those sentences applied to his own work as well as the historic creeds. Recognizing the presence of this attitude helps us understand why no official creeds or doctrinal statements have ever been put forward as tests of fellowship.

Recounting the distinction between traditionalism and tradition serves as a useful reminder of what should be the Church of God movement's attitude toward its own past as well as that of all Christendom. Thus we have seen already something of the movement's ideas about authority, especially in the theological arena.

II

Having established a stance toward our history, we need to consider what we mean by the word *authority*. In so doing we will need to shift the focus of our conversation from matters of theology to those of polity. We do well to do that, because such a move will help us grasp the point that theology really has to do with life, and when it loses that touch theology isn't worth much at all.

In most of our discussions we associate the word authority with the idea of power. Commonly, we think that the idea of authority means the power or ability to coerce action or compliance. Typically, if some person has been placed in authority, we understand him or her to possess the responsibility that accompanies being "in charge." Authorities are those who see to it that work get done.

Stanley Hauerwas asserts that "authority is fundamentally a political-moral concept. Therefore, its meaning is dependent upon an understanding of the nature of human community and the moral good" (1986:39). If his assertion is correct, then our common definition of authority as power says a great deal about the kind of community we think the church is; for to think of authority as power suggests that we think that the church is an organization wherein the presence of some weakness requires a compensatory authority or power to offset that weakness or inability. We might call this the "deficiency theory" of authority, a theory that, incidentally, undergirds the corporate bureaucratic mentality of our age.

In the deficiency theory, authority resides in offices or position rather than in persons or the community. When one leaves office, his or her authority remains behind. While this theory of authority may be a useful model for national politics or a corporation like General Motors, one may legitimately question whether such an understanding of authority is acceptable for the church. On the whole I think that to think of authority in the church as power and that, therefore, more or better organization is the solution to our problems is a serious mistake. Historically the Church of God movement has been skeptical of the merits of organization. That skepticism has served to keep our organization from being any more authoritarian and bureaucratic than it already is. To what might we attribute this fortunate turn of events? I think the fact that we have relatively little bureaucracy stems from important theological insights into the nature and practice of church.

The deficiency theory of authority turns out to have roots in ancient Roman political thought, and this idea was quite at odds with biblical ideas about authority. To point out these differences, the use of two Latin versions of the word *auctores* will be necessary, words from which our word *authority* derives. *Auctoritas*, in Roman politics, signified the authority of those who always point back to the foundation. "Once something has been founded it remains binding on all generations . . . Those endowed with authority . . . obtained it by descent and by transmission from those who had laid the foundations for all things to come, the ancestors . . . The authority of the living was always derived, depending upon . . . the authority of the founders" (Brown 1985:21).

A second idea of authority, one that Delwin Brown believes is in keeping with the Hebrew Bible, is denoted by the word *auctor*, from which we get the word "author." "In religion," says Brown, "that which is authoritative is that which authors. It is that which gives life" (27). The analogy of the parent-child relationship may be a useful illustration here. The parents create ("author") the child, and in the child's early years of development they exercise great influence over the development of his or her character. This character gradually takes on a life of its own, however, even to the point at which it begins shaping lives of its authors. Authority in this sense is not coercive power; it is life-giving, enabling creativity.[2]

Recall now my opening remarks about the function of history in the life of the church. In theology, *auctoritas* is the authority at work in what we labeled traditionalism. *Auctor* is that authority at work in tradition. But what will *auctor* look like in the political life of the church?

The answer to this question requires us to lay aside the idea of the church as institution or management unit in favor of considering the church as a practice. This may not be as difficult or confusing as it sounds, since C. E. Brown already made that distinction when he said we could organize the work of the church but not the church itself. I interpret Brown to mean that church as institution signifies the organized work of the church. But the work is not the church, which really is a set of practices (worship, prayer, fellowship, study, and the like) and which are beyond our capacity to organize in any coercive way. The practice of church will naturally lead to the work of the institutional church. We may properly suspect the quality of those practices when no work is forthcoming. But the institutional work of the church depends upon the prior practice of church. In that practice lies the heart of the Christian community.

The institutional work of the church sustains the practice of church, but it also tends to corrupt it. Although ministers preach and lead worship, intrinsic practices of the church, for the joy that is their chief internal good, money will also have to be provided. A building that can house the practices of prayer, worship, and education must also be secured. Money and buildings require trustees or deacons for their collection and management. Trustees are important for the work of the church, and their activity sustains the practice of church. But their activity provides goods, like money and buildings, external to the practice of church. Ministers take money for preaching or leading worship or working with the youth, but that is not the reason they engage in these practices. If money ever becomes their reason, then their ministerial practice has been corrupted.

If we may distinguish between the church as the practicing of faith and the institutional work of the church, then we may be able to see a bit more clearly the danger inherent in allowing the organizational model of authority to became our operative understanding of authority in the life of the church. Organizational authority may be necessary to accomplish certain tasks, but these tasks must never be mistaken for the church as practice and the kind of authority that pertains to practices. I am suggesting that *auctor* is the notion of authority that pertains to the church at its heart, in its practices. In the case of practices, "authority is not required because human beings lack something. . . . Rather, it derives from common participation in worthy endeavors" (Haverwas 1986:44).

> Authority is needed, according to (Yves) Simon, because "it is desirable that particular goods should be taken care of by particular agencies, . . . Since those goods are not known by necessity, but must be discovered through concrete judgments, authority is essential for the pursuit of the common good (Hauerwas 1986:45-46).

Authority in a practice or set of practices is not a matter of power or a special knowledge or ability privately held by the person in charge. Churchly authority is more on the order of "authoring." It is creative and enabling. It helps us know better that which is common knowledge—or at least available to us all. In this sense authority is not the correlative of coercive power but of wisdom and judgment.

III

With all this theoretical material as background, let us now turn to the question of authority as we have handled it in the history of the Church of God movement. It is fair to say that authorities in both senses have been described above. Those who have exercised authority as *auctoritas* came to be identified primarily as managers or people in charge. Those who were more *auctor* in their idea of authority we might describe as "sages" or wise people. Now the case is probably that many, if not the vast majority, of our leader types embodied both styles of authority. But I also think that certain people in the movement and certain of our activities have been ordered more to one style than the other, even if not exclusively.

Clearly we have had figures who conceived their authority as *auctoritas*. They tended to be managers who were considered to be in charge. One of the best examples of this authoritarian style is E. E. Byrum, the second editor of the *Gospel Trumpet*. When Byrum succeeded D. S. Warner, managerial authority replaced charismatic leadership, as the late Gale Hetrick observed (1980:105). To be sure, Byrum's authoritarianism rested in both his personality and the circumstances that surrounded his leadership. The youthful movement, faced with theological and organizational crisis, seemed to require a strong, forceful authority. Byrum was, by virtue of office, that person, and his *auctoritas* was virtually without challenge. When heterodox teaching on sanctification surfaced in 1898-99, Byrum summarily excommunicated those who would not recant their differences. He exercised sole authority over the status of the ministry; as editor he recognized ministers to be in good standing or else out of fellowship. But centralized authoritarian leadership eventually proved to be E. E. Byrum's undoing.

Byrum of course was succeeded by F. G. Smith, who had served as his personal secretary at the Gospel Trumpet Company. According to Robert Reardon, C. Lowrey Quinn once asked Smith for some advice out of his own experience on life in the church. How had Smith come to be editor at the age of thirty-five? Smith answered, "I got in line and I stayed in line" (1979:45). That terse sentence clearly indicates what Smith had learned about authority from Byrum.

Smith served concurrently as editor and chair of the missionary board. Prior to his succession of Byrum, the movement's mission in India had already grown into a flourishing church. The leadership of that church was primarily Indian—A. D. Khan, R. N. Mundul, Mosir Moses and J. J. M. Roy. Added to this group of bright, aggressive men was the sympathetic and intellectually gifted ministry of missionary George Tasker. The Indian church grew significantly before the arrival of American missionaries, and Tasker was wise enough to get out of the way of the gifted Indian church leaders, one of whom—A. D. Khan—became his great friend. Because Tasker did not share Editor Smith's church-historical exegesis of the Apocalypse, the latter viewed him as theologically suspect. For his part, Tasker (and Khan, for that matter) interpreted the movement's emphasis on itself as the church of the evening light as but a new form of the very sectarian spirit it originally had protested. In 1923 Smith sent Floyd W. Heinly out to India as field secretary with the assignment to bring the church there in line. Heinly faithfully carried out this task but with disastrous consequences for the Indian church and mission.

My intent here is not to impugn F. G. Smith's motives or integrity. He acted in precisely the same manner as E. E. Byrum had during the Anti-cleansing crisis. But this episode illustrates a common conception of authority in the movement, especially prevalent, I think, among those who by personality or assignment become managers or, worse, "CEOs."[3] As stated above, this is a "deficiency theory" of authority; it conceives authority as the power to compensate for the group's weakness. Not unlike his mentor Byrum, in 1930 Smith left the editor's office due in part to the misgivings of some that he had too much power—or at least that he was representing himself as having more power than he should or, in fact did, possess.

Byrum and Smith are but two examples of authoritarian leaders. Many others could be listed: C. S. Sisler and William "Dad" Hartman in Michigan, C. E. Byers and R. C. Caudill in Ohio, E. A. Reardon in Chicago. These were people accustomed to being in charge, who thought that authority was a synonym for power and who used that power to accomplish the tasks that needed to be done. From the perspective of the person who holds *auctoritas*, this seems the way things should be. It seems to offer us the efficiency that is so highly prized in our culture. But does *auctoritas* have as much attraction for us when we envisage ourselves on the receiving rather than the giving end of authoritarian action?

Contemporary with Byrum and Smith was a woman whose extraordinary ministry exemplified an authority more in keeping with the notion of authoring or *auctor*. I am referring of course to Nora Hunter, whose ministry spanned a period from the 1890s to the 1950s. "Madame President" was a principal figure in the organization of the group we now know as Women of the Church of God. Before that, Hunter served as pastor, evangelist, gospel worker, and supervisor of children in the home at Grand Junction, Michigan.

A reviewer of Hunter's life, and especially her style of leadership, will be struck, I think, by the absence of the idea of authority as *auctoritas*. For Nora Hunter's authority, which was great indeed, rested on the practices of the church rather than office or appeals to the founders or some other way of holding power. Consequently, it was not important for Hunter to appear to be in charge or to have the power to get things done. That does not, of course, mean that nothing got done during her tenure as president of the women's organization. Quite to the contrary, at a time of deep financial crisis, Hunter succeeded in galvanizing the missionary effort of the church, and this on the slenderest of resources. She accomplished this feat not by being "in charge" and coercing people, but by recognizing the talents of others and encouraging them to develop their gifts. They grew in her *auctor* style of leadership and eventually went beyond her. Such is the nature of *auctor*.[4]

IV

The principle of authority manifested in the ideal of *auctor* is grounded in a set of practices central to the life of the church. This means that authority resides in a person of those practices rather than an occupant of a particular office. Because, in the Church of God movement, those practices are so much a part of our polity or way of being together, we may move to a concluding discussion of the importance of the fact that, for us, authority is bound up in the community of faith.

In an illuminating essay entitled "The Hermeneutics of Peoplehood," the Mennonite theologian John Howard Yoder discusses the radical reformation's understanding and practice of church (1984). This understanding, resting as it does on the conviction that the church is a voluntary association of those who believe unto salvation on the Lord Jesus Christ, lifts up the idea of church as a community that "can affirm individual dignity . . . without enshrining individualism. They can likewise realize community without authorizing lordship or establishment" (24). In other words, in the view of the believers' churches, the community of faith possesses the authority of *auctor* rather than *auctoritas*. Moreover, Yoder claims, this authority is grounded in the church's very polity. Yoder makes several claims about this way of being together:

(1) The church will have "agents of direction" in its midst. Citing 1 Corinthians 14:3, 29, Yoder identifies preaching's role as the stater and reinforcer of "a vision of the place of the believing community in history, which vision locates moral reasoning" (29). This vision rises out of the community's narrative as the people of God continuous with that narrative that starts, "In the beginning, God . . ." As such, the vision offered in preaching points us toward the goal toward which the community grows corporately and individually, the measure of the stature of the fullness of Christ.

(2) Citing Matthew 13:52, Yoder says that the community of faith also requires "agents of memory," those skilled at the interpretation and exposition of the Scripture, "the store par excellence of treasures old and new" (31).

(3) The teacher also is a guide for the community of faith (1984:32). The teacher, according to Yoder, is one who follows the advice given to Timothy to maintain the delicate balance between retaining "the pattern of sound words" and "avoid disputing about words," (cf. 2 Tim. 1:13; 2:16) (P. 32).

(4) Last, Yoder says that the "community will be guided by agents of order and due process" (33). These are the men

and women "whose function is to assure the wholesome process of the entire group, rather than some prerogatives of their own" (33).

What Yoder has outlined here, of course, are the various responsibilities of the church's ministry. But he has described the ministry in such a way that we see that it serves rather than manages the church. The *community* deliberates; the ministry guides, remembers, discerns and ensures fairness in the community's all-important deliberation of the implications of Scripture for us and therefore the kind of people God is calling us to be.

Episodes in our recent history demonstrate precisely this believers' way of being the church and the *auctor* entailed in such a polity. We may look to the recent dialogue on internal unity and the meetings of the commission on glossolalia as splendid examples not only of Yoder's analysis, but more important clear examples of the Church of God way of being the church. They are our very polity. Sad to say, we seem to practice this polity best only when crisis threatens rather than as our normal way of being together.

We might also look to the early ordination practices of the movement. There we would find great reliance on the authorization for ministry in the charismatic gifting of men and women. But we should be careful not to think that such are examples of the individual's acquisition of *auctoritas*. People could not simply announce that they were ordained ministers, for finally the community made a judgment about the quality and authenticity of a person's gifts. While true that the Holy Spirit calls to ministry through charismatic gifting, it is equally true that ministers in the movement were recognized as such by the community, corporately and in the early practice of senior ministers vouching for the minister newly included in the clergy list. Neither managerial expertise nor authoritarian power is sufficient to this task. Rather, the wisdom and judgment implicit in discernment are the gifts upon which the community relies in confirming those who say they are called to ministry.

In this essay I have tried to distinguish the authority of *auctor* from that of *auctoritas*, and I have not hid my preference for the former. That preference rests upon several observations. *Auctor* seems to be that view of authority that is present in God's relations with the world and in the church at its best. *Auctoritas*, on the other hand, displays the authority of the corporate model of bureaucracy, whether business or government. The idea of authority resident in *auctor* will foster the moral development of men and women in the church in such ways that they become interdependent on one another rather than dependent on those in charge. Indeed, the authority of *auctor* calls into question the very legitimacy of a leadership style that tells people what to do.

While an Anderson College undergraduate, I took a course in Old Testament with Dr. Gus Jeeninga. His suggestion about the manner of the composition of some of the Proverbs was one of the lessons of that course, and it is suggestive of the role of wisdom and community in the idea of *auctor* that I have tried to display. Some of the proverbs seem to have come into being as the collective effort of elders seated about the village council. Someone might launch the group's conversation by stating the topic—"a soft answer." Numerous attempts at expounding that idea might have been offered before consensus approved the one we have—"turns away wrath." Similarly, it seems to me, we can conceive authority as the collective role of the community of faith deliberating the all-important question of how it will live as the people of God. This task calls forth the best wisdom from each of us, but it will lift the role of the leader as sage over that of manager.

The history of the Church of God holds examples of people and practices of authority in which wisdom and the sage clearly were prized. That same history yields examples of those who thought authority was a matter of power and managerial expertise. Although the church surely must value the goods of efficiency so prized by this latter conception of authority, we must always remember that *auctoritas* tends to forget those goods of excellence that must circumscribe its drive to accomplish its assignment. In our urgent desire to get the job done, we must remember that the job must be done for the right reasons and in the right manner.

Thus authority in the Church of God can be about managers, CEOs, and being in charge. But on the other hand, it can be about sages, wisdom, and the community's deliberations and life. Because of the kind of people and the quality of fellowship produced in the latter, and because it seems more faithful to the biblical vision of God's care and nurture of creation, Israel, and the church, I think the practice of authority as *auctor* by a community of wisdom and remembrance describes the way we can live together at our best, which is to say according to a polity that will help the world to believe that God sent Jesus to redeem it.

Chapter 6 Notes

1. An important note here is that I take for granted that in the Church of God movement, theology's authority is grounded in the Bible. Persons within the movement have surely disagreed (and I think that this disagreement is on balance healthy) over the *manner* of the Bible's authority for the church's theology. But I know of no Church of God writer, living or dead, who thinks that the Bible is not authoritative for theological reflection. So when we ask about authority for theology, we are inquiring into the warrants we have for saying what we think, and what it is that makes some statements more authoritative than others.

2. The difference be *auctoritas* and *auctor* is illustrated in the following story. When a teen-ager living on his parents' farm outside Drake, North Dakota, my father had permission to drive his father's car to and from high school. That was the extent of the permission—to and from school. Once some adventurous friends of his suggested that he drive them all over to Balfour (which, being even smaller than Drake, could not have been worth the risk) during the school lunch hour. They promised to buy gasoline to replace what the trip would use, so that "no one would ever know."

133

To this day, when my father tells that story the final sentence of it still carries a note of moral outrage: "*I* would know." There in the schoolyard at lunchtime, my father was beyond the reach of his parent's *auctoritas*. But my grandfather and grandmother's *auctor* had enabled my father to grow into the kind of person who did not require the immediate presence of authoritarian power or coercion.

3. The term *CEO* (Corporate Executive Officer) is appropriate in the world of the bureaucratic corporation. But I can think of no more unfortunate misapplication of that term than to the leadership of the body of Christ, the church, or any of its agencies or individual districts or congregations. Such an application trains us to see the church as corporation and that vision legitimizes a polity quite out of keeping with such Pauline passages as 1 Corinthians 12 or Romans 12:1-16.

4. I am reminded of two of my high school teachers. One of them never tired of telling us he was in charge, a speech we heard initially on the first day of the school year. He repeatedly told us what he would do to us were we ever to forget that he was in charge. Of course, the fact that he had to give this speech frequently and at a louder and louder volume belied his claim to authority. On the other hand, another of our teachers never said the first word about being in charge, nor did he ever need to make such claims. He was for us, and his efforts to enable our growth as students and young men and women demonstrated him to be the authority (*auctor*) that he in fact was.

In addition to the works cited in this essay, I am listing the following resources that have also influenced my thinking on this and related topics:

Berkhof, Hendrik
1962 *Christ and the Powers.* Scottdale: Herald Press.

Hauerwas, Stanley
1988 "Clerical Character: Reflecting on Ministerial Morality." In *Christian Existence Today: Essays on Church, World and Living In Between.* Durham, NC: Labyrinth Press

MacIntyre, Alasdair
1988 *Whose Justice? Which Rationality?* Notre Dame: University of Notre Dame Press.
1984 *After Virtue*, 2nd Edition. Notre Dame: University of Notre Dame Press.

McClendon, James W., Jr.
1986 *Systematic Theology*, vol. I, *Ethics.* Nashville: Abingdon Press.

Sykes, Stephen
1984 *The Identity of Christianity.* Philadelphia: Fortress Press.

Yoder, John Howard
1972 *The Politics of Jesus.* Grand Rapids: William B. Eerdmans Publishing Co.

History as a Moral and Political Art

Remember the days of old,
  Think of the generations of long ago;
  Ask your father to recount it
  and your elders to tell you the tale.
        —Deuteronomy 32:7 (NEB)

euteronomy was written, in part, to rekindle the communal memory of a people who had lost touch with its story. Ritual had lost the rich narrative context that gave meaning to acts of worship. Torah had become a rigid legal code rather than instruction in the way of the Lord. In response to Divine guidance, Israel no longer delighted in the word of life but could offer only a desiccated obedience. More than a mere exercise in nostalgia, the act of remembering served the important functions of helping Israel to understand again who they were as a people and the kind of people Yahweh was calling them to be. The act of "remembering the days of old" thus served moral and political ends.

The sixth chapter of Deuteronomy treats the problem of Israel, now in the Promised Land of Canaan but having forgotten the story of how it got there. In this chapter an unnamed parent is confronted by a child who had never learned the meaning of Torah for the life of the people Israel; thus the question, "What is the meaning of the testimonies and the statutes and ordinances which the Lord our God has commanded you?" (6:20). A generation had arisen in Israel that was illiterate in the traditions that told the story of how the mighty acts of God brought its people into being.

It is instructive that the anonymous parent of Deuteronomy 6 is told to answer the child's question by reciting an abridged narrative account of the Exodus. Characteristic of the Old Testament is the awareness that such questions as "Who are we?" and "What is the meaning and purpose of our existence?" must be answered through narrative. For Israel, to be the people of God required that they remember the narrative by which they had found and negotiated their way as the people of Yahweh in the world.

This vignette from Deuteronomy illustrates the Old Testament's deep indebtedness to narrative for its politics and morality. To remember was both a political and a moral art, for the act of remembering was a principal ingredient in their polity, i.e., their way of being together. Moreover as a people, through remembering they learned what kind of people God was calling them to be. The Hebrew emphasis on remembering through narrative, and the significance of this art for morality and politics merits our consideration as the contemporary people of God. Christians of the late twentieth century ought to consider how the writing, reading, and recitation of narrative history indispensably contribute to the moral formation of the Christian community.

The most important function of the historian's craft is its contribution to the present and future. For Christians, historical narrative, by its recounting of the ways in which we have come to be the kind of church we now are, contributes directly to what ought to be an ongoing conversation that deliberates the question, "What kind of people is God calling us to be?" This question is, of course, about our character and, therefore, a moral consideration of the first importance. That such a conversation constitutes our community means that we also are engaged in politics.[1] Both the Apostle Paul and the philosopher Aristotle before him understood the deep connections between our characters and our communities.[2]

These are not popular ideas at this point in the life of the United States, given its very strong commitment to individualism. Many excellent books and articles examine this phenomenon, and some of them treat its deep impact on American religion in general and Christianity specifically,[3] In a culture that celebrates doing "your own thing" because "I gotta be me" it is small wonder that we are glad "I did it my way." Americans scarcely recognize or admit to the presence of the stout cords that bind our moral growth to the groups of which we are parts.

Indeed individualism runs so deep in our society that we think of individuals as the ultimate unit of society. In such thinking the group is constituted by individuals, whereas in other cultures the individual is regarded as an extension of the group. This latter view, one may add, is characteristic of the Bible. Thus the Apostle Paul claims that the church is the body of Christ and that individuals are members of this body. Women and men do not constitute the body; they are extensions of it.

On this matter of individualism one may consider the great distance between contemporary Americans and people of the ancient world by comparing their respective attitudes on the punishment of exile. To the ancients, the sentence to exile meant a fate worse than death. In fact Socrates preferred an unjust death sentence to the escape and voluntary exile proposed by his friends. Exile meant severance from the community in which one was morally nourished and sustained, and that severance would relegate the person to the status of nonentity. Quite to the contrary, modern American individualists, while no doubt feeling loss and separation in exile, would not be inclined to think that separation from their community signified the end of their existence, that it was worse than death.

The strident individualism of modern America only obscures the deep connections between our individual character and the communities of which we are parts. Family systems therapy is telling us of the ways in which our selves are formed by the interpersonal dynamics of the family group.

This is but one example of the strong relationship between the "self-in-relation," as Richard Bondi described character and the groups that shape it.

James McLendon explores this relationship in his treatment of Dietrich Bonhoeffer's lost commitment to pacifism. Few German Lutherans embraced pacifism during the second world war, and so Bonhoeffer was something of an oddity and without theological or religious support from the broader German community. But Bonhoeffer shaped the Confessing church seminary at Finkenwalde, the seminary over which he presided, into a group capable of sustaining one another's pacifist commitments. In time the Nazi government closed the Finkenwalde community, drafting the students and thereby dispersing them. Bonhoeffer returned to his parental home in Berlin and in the process reentered a socio-political circle for whom violence was a legitimate means of achieving worthy ends. This exchange of one community for another of very different moral assumptions weakened Bonhoeffer's pacifism and paved the way for him to conspire against Hitler. The conspiracy failed, of course, and Bonhoeffer was hanged only days before the war's end in Europe. McLendon labels Bonhoeffer's life a tragedy, but not so much because of the execution of this promising young pastor-theologian. Bonhoeffer died tragically because he, along with other Christians in Germany, "had no effective [social] moral structure in the church that was adequate to the crucial need of church and German people alike. . . . No structures, no practices, no skills of political life existed that were capable of resisting, Christianly resisting, the totalitarianism of the times" (1986:207).

McLendon's observations about Dietrich Bonhoeffer and the church in Germany may be applied to the church in the United States as well. To the degree that we think of the church as an aggregation of individuals, we come to lose whatever social and political skills we may once have had. The church is a congregation, which means that its members must understand themselves in light of, as parts of, this body that is greater than the sum of its parts. Such a conception rests, in part, on our awareness that when we become part of the church, our individual lives are joined to the long, long story of a people who began their journey with God in a book called *Genesis.*

Insofar as groups are sustained by a narrative account, they are morally significant for they are the political expression of values embedded in those narratives. Of course the Enlightenment liberal political philosophy upon which the American political experiment rests denies the importance of tradition for present and future. But even the characters of antitraditional Enlightened liberals are formed by a tradition.[4] In other words, just because you say you have or need no story does not mean that you have one.

In our society adults tend to think that stories are for the young or intellectually immature. Children may be entertained by stories, or they may divert for a few hours the rational minds of adults. But the fact that we commonly refer to a narrative as "just a story" suggests our real attitude. Somehow we have come to the mistaken notion that stories are always tall tales and never true. This leads to a preference for the rational, the didactic, and the infamous "bottom line." In this we fail to see that the narrative account of the journey already is part of the conclusion and therefore incapable of reduction to rational propositions or simple moralistic "lessons."

Despite our refusal to acknowledge the influence of narrative and community on our moral growth, in this essay I wish to explore the impact of historical narrative on morality and politics, with specific reference to Christianity and the church. The plan for proceeding is quite simple; it is organized around very basic questions: What do we mean by "history?" What is morality? What is politics? How does the narrative art of the historian touch them?

I hope that it will be clear that by linking history and morality I do not mean that we are free to ransack the past for lessons to be moralistically applied to our own time and space. While we should learn from history, we ought studiously to shun the phrase "history teaches." To avoid that phrase, however, is not to conclude that our efforts to reconstruct and understand the past have no moral impact. But what is it we mean by morality?

I

Moral philosophy recently has taken up an old theme of ethics, namely, the idea of virtue. Many lay people might be surprised to learn that this word ever disappeared from the vocabularies of philosophers and theologians. Without going into a lengthy account of how this came to be, let me say that in the last two decades, the idea of virtue has been making a comeback in moral philosophy.[5]

Classical Greeks understood virtue (*arete*) to be the quality of persons or objects that enabled them to fulfill their purpose. The purpose of a knife is to cut, and its virtue therefore is the keenness of its blade. Consequently a dull knife may be said to have lost its virtue. Another way of thinking about virtue concerns skill, although we must qualify this notion. In much the same way that we can master the skill of riding a bicycle, we can be trained in the virtues. Training in the virtues does not mean, however, that, once trained, we will always act in a virtuous manner reflexively, in some robot-like way. Nor does the conception of virtue as a skill entail the elimination of deliberation and reflection. The virtues we may have acquired must still be employed in an intentional, thoughtful manner. Virtuous actions must be justifiable by good reasons and practical wisdom.

Virtues are embodied in a person's character. By this latter term I mean, simply enough, the kind of person we are. One usage of character means to honor a person as in "John has character!" or "Mary is a woman of high character." In these statements character is a synonym for "good person." But I mean by character that element of the human personality that enables us to predict how a person is likely to act. Thus when we say, "You can always count on Mary," we have said something about the kind of person that Mary is, namely, that she is reliable. If we say that John is unpredictable, we still have said something about his character: John is predictably unpredictable. So human beings both good and bad possess character. The term should not be applied only to the honorable or morally distinguished.

Character shapes our vision of the world. The way we see the world is of crucial importance to our morality. In fact, "our moral existence can be taken seriously only when the vision developed out of an individual's experience and vision is comprehended."⁶ Yet, we do not all see the same world. Where one person sees death and despair another sees resurrection and hope. Is either vision accurate or are both simply projections of different characters, one a pessimist and the other an optimist? Is what we see solely a function of personality, or must our characters incorporate a training to see the world as it really is?

Christian character includes the capacity to see the world as under the reign of God. This is no easy task, for much around us denies this lordship. Nevertheless Christians learn to see the world differently, and they believe their vision of the world conforms to reality. This training in vision is an inescapable component of a virtue ethics.

So vision and virtues are expressions of a particular kind of character. This is more than a claim about "personality differences," for our characters develop within and through a set of relationships that we may call our community. By this term I mean something far more than a geographical locale or a fellowship group. Community is not something human beings "have" or "build." The word ought never to be used in this adjectival sense. *For a community is an extended conversation about the meaning and implications of its constitutive narratives for the lives of its members.*

This definition of community challenges our typical belief that a good community is a place or gathering where all persons present are happy and like one another. While it is likely that communities will experience periods, perhaps even extended ones, of harmony, it will also be the case that communities are arenas of ferment and disagreement, perhaps even argument. St. Paul's autobiographical section in the letter to the Galatians includes an account of his confrontation with the Apostle Peter over the controversial status of Gentiles in the young Christian movement. This was no light or peripheral issue. It was a question that grew directly out of the life story of Jesus of Nazareth. So when Paul says he got in Peter's face (to make a contemporary paraphrase), we are being told that these two men were engaged in a vigorous debate about the implications of the gospel story for their lives in the church.

This is a marvelous example of the Christian community in action, and it is worth a parenthetical observation that, despite their deep disagreement and, perhaps, anger, these men did not excommunicate one another nor did either of them go into schism. They apparently were not prepared to sin against love even though they strongly disagreed. Despite serious, legitimate differences over its implications, both Peter and Paul remained within the circle of love that rested upon the same narrative.

The story of Peter and Paul's confrontation illustrates the idea of a community as an extended conversation, even at times an argument. This further suggests that people who undertake efforts to prevent such conversation or argument in the name of keeping the peace are misguided. In one sense attempts to preserve tranquility at all costs are immoral, for they only serve to frustrate the group in its attempt to answer the question of what kind of people we will be, i.e., the question of character. Hence the leaders of narrative-based communities ought to make it their business to encourage such conversations rather than inhibit them. But the conversation that forms community will not be idle or based simply in anyone's opinion. The narratives out of which the community arises must provide the basis for our conversation.

The communities of which we are a part profoundly shape the development of our characters. At a time when popular Freudianism falsely believes that any such influence is necessarily repressive, Christians, if not others, must insist that the expectations of our communities that we will grow up to

144

possess specific virtues in certain characters is not all bad. In this regard Edmund Pincoffs refers to "communities of expectation" and about them he says, "Aristotle did not give open lectures; St. Paul did not write open letters. When they used the word 'we,' they spoke from within a community of expectations and ideals: a community within which character was cultivated" (1986:34).

The expectations and ideals of a community rise out of its formative traditions or narratives. Communities are extended conversations, not idle chit-chat groups. The conversation is *about* something and that something is a story. By story I do not mean tale, but a narrative that explains the community in the wider realm in general. Out of this narrative the ideals and expectations of a community arise, for within this narrative, members of the community hear smaller stories about villains and heroes, their vices and virtues, and how to tell the difference. Through the recounting and hearing of a community's constitutive narratives, its members come to some idea of the qualities that are embodied in a good person.

James Sanders' description of the canonical process illustrates the manner in which narratives constitute the conversation that is the biblical community. The heritage of the people of God is a collection of stories (we may call them "traditions" as well as narratives) about God's dealings with the world. These traditions display certain characteristics: they are stable and yet adaptable, multivalent, and capable of repetition and resignification. The presence of such characteristics requires a community struggling to understand its identity and purpose as the people of God. Sanders is adamant on the point that the biblical canons are not the product of solitary individuals. Rather, the canons are the result of the struggle of the community, the people of God, to understand itself. The name for this effort to understand one's situation in light of an earlier teaching is, in the Hebrew, *midrash* (24).

Much in the manner of *midrash*, contemporary Christian communities draw upon the narratives of their past for insight into present dilemmas and struggles. These narratives may at points conflict, for they represent the stories of various perspectives and constituencies. So much the better, for as Sanders says of a similar biblical diversity,

> No one person, no denomination, no theology, and certainly no ideology can exhaust the Bible or claim its *unity*. It bears with its own redeeming contradictions, and this is a major reason it has lasted so long and has spoken so effectively to so many different historical contexts and communities. Once a theme or strain or thread rightly perceived in the Bible has been isolated and absolutized, it simply becomes available for challenge from another theme or strain also there. The whole Bible, of whichever canon, can never be stuffed into one theological box, as is classically recognized by the term *biblical paradox*: the canon always contains the seed of redemption of any abuse of it (37).

I wish to claim that in the same way that the diverse traditions of scripture produce a canonical community called the people of God, the ongoing narratives—that which we call post-biblical history—ought to produce a historical community called the church. Of course I am not claiming canonical status for the history of Christianity. But I am suggesting that a similar pattern of inquiring exchange with a multiplicity of post-biblical narratives contributes to the moral life of the churches, especially in their particularist or denominational expressions. Such an exchange enables us to understand how our forefathers and foremothers struggled with their attempts to apply biblical wisdom and insights to everyday life. To know something of their struggles cannot but help us in our effort to understand the implications of the gospel story for our own lives.

This way of envisaging the relation of narratives and their community amounts to an appeal for the church's attitude toward its history to be somewhat analogous to what some have termed the "midrashic attitude." As Roger LeDeaut says of this attitude:

> Midrashic instruction can be compared with the manna with which Moses nourished Israel in the desert (Targum to Eccl. 12:11). If it is impossible to define midrash, it is because it has known an immense popularity, as a part of Jewish *life* and as a part of the sphere of the existential which refuses to be conceptualized, where it is first of all the response to the question: What does Scripture want to say for the life of today? (1971:259-282).

The community called the church retells the narratives that have shaped it. It asks of these narratives, "What have these stories to say to us? How can we understand the present and the future in their light? How do these stories reflect our understanding, past and present, of Scripture? What signals do we find in them for the direction of our lives?" But these narratives are the privileged possession of no single person or party in the church. Thus the community of faith is required to be nothing less than a multi-tiered conversation with each other, the Scripture, and Christian history. Out of this conversation come our perceptions of the kind of people God is calling us to be.

The constitutive narrative for the Greeks was the material collected in the *Iliad* and the *Odyssey*. The strong, warlike, nimble-witted Odysseus, the hero of the latter of these epic poems, embodies the virtues that the Greeks thought were part of the character of a good human being. Similarly, the Apostle Paul refers his beloved Philippian brothers and sisters to the gospel narrative. The virtues of a Roman citizen in the first century scarcely resembled those of a Christian. Thus Paul reminded the Philippians that their citizenship was in heaven. They belonged no longer to Rome, but to a community founded on a story quite unlike the Roman narrative of military conquest and the power of the juggernaut. Therefore, Paul says, "Let this mind be in you that was also in Christ" and then in Philippians 2:5-11 he describes the goal or *telos* of Christian moral growth by referring to Jesus as the one who embodies the virtues that compose the church's understanding of the good human being. In other words, the Christian community, founded on the story of Jesus, should expect its citizens to develop morally in the virtues of Christ rather than the virtues of Rome based, as the latter were, in a very different narrative.

It may have become apparent to some readers by now that defining virtue, vision, community, and character as I have means that I must think that morality is community dependent, that our notions of virtue, good, and evil rise out of the narratives that form our communities. The person who has reached these conclusions will want to know, then, whether it is possible for us to make comparative judgments about the narratives and virtues of respective communities. Is there any way we can say that the morality of community A is superior to that of community B? Or can we say no more than "these moralities and communities are different?"

So long as we are within the time and space we call history, we will always see through a glass darkly. Nevertheless it is possible to compare narratives and their communities and to make judgments about their relative merits. This judgment rests upon the abilities of communities to resist the temptation to use violence in their defense and also upon the degree to which they are able to tell the truth about themselves.

Stanley Hauerwas says that "a 'truth' that must use violence to secure its existence cannot be truth" (1983:15). If a community is founded on true narratives, it will not need to resort to violence to defend itself or make itself safe. Somehow it is utterly contradictory to think that the truthfulness of our ideals depends upon our ability to coerce others to accept them. Communities founded upon narratives that either permit or even glorify the use of violence must be judged as less than truthful and good. More than the good and the truth they advocate, such communities trust violence.

Such misplaced trust renders their moralities suspect.

Good and truthful stories also will enable communities to escape the temptation to self deception and thus enable them to hear and tell the truth. Good and truthful stories allow us to remember the bad along with the good. In this manner we avoid the slavish adherence to the past that Jaroslav Pelikan labels "traditionalism." This attitude he sums up as the "dead faith of the living" (1985:65). Those who regard the past from this point of view make an idol of it and believe that all change necessarily deviates from the past norm. Of necessity, they also remember only the good. But Pelikan contends that one may approach the past not as traditionalism but as tradition, which is the "living faith of the dead" (65). The present carries the past within it. Christians of tradition recognize this fact and allow the people of the past to exercise their vote in the question of what kind of people God is calling us to be. People of tradition have regard for the past without being enslaved by it. They understand, perhaps welcome, the continuity that ties together the present with the whole past and the future. Tradition enables us to live therefore from memory to hope. Moreover, to deny people this continuity is to leave them without the bearings to negotiate the dangerous journey we call life. For as Alasdair MacIntyre says:

> I can only answer the question 'What am I to do?' if I can answer the prior question 'Of what story or stories do I find myself a part?" We enter human society, that is, with one or more imputed characters—roles into which we have been drafted—and we have to learn what they are in order to be able to understand how others respond to us and how our responses are apt to be construed. It is through hearing stories about wicked stepmothers, lost children, good but misguided kings . . . youngest sons who waste their inheritance on riotous living and go into exile to live with the swine, that children learn or mislearn both what a child and what a parent is,

what the cast of characters may be in the drama into which they have been born and what the ways of the world are. Deprive children of stories and you leave them unscripted, anxious stutterers in their actions as in their words" (1984:211-216 *passim*).

II

For some time now historians have worried that their field of study is disintegrating. For a long time "history" meant a narrative account of nations, or civilizations, dominated by political events. Then a "new history" came along to inform historians that this narrative and political approach was old and needed to be replaced by new approaches and methodologies. The new history was interested in analysis and causation rather than narrative writing, and it replaced the "old history's" political theme with social ones. Thus we have histories of private life, the family, popular culture, sexual practices, and so forth. This "new history" has firmly entrenched itself in the academic study of history in American colleges and universities.

Lately new historians have begun to wonder, however, whether their field is not being reduced to the categories that have supplied them with their methodologies, e.g., anthropology, sociology, demography, and so forth. Talk has begun of the need for a "new old history," one that returns to narrative form and political concerns but is expanded to include the wealth of information discovered through the methods of social history.

All of this may surprise the nonspecialist reader who always thought he or she knew what history was, i.e., the study of the past. But there is more. Historians also disagree on the nature of their audience. Some argue that they write history for specialists in the field. Others contend that history should be written so that nonspecialists can read, appreciate, and benefit from it. These latter historians are often referred to by the former as "popularizers" and by that term no compliment is intended. But then the "popularizers" think of their adversaries as "elitists," and that can hardly be praise in an egalitarian democracy.

Beyond the question of audience there also exist the questions of historical "objectivity," and the purpose for writing history. Historians, as Gertrude Himmelfarb says, are informed and inspired by the ideal of writing just exactly what really happened, but that ideal always eludes individuals (1987:21). The historian's work cannot meet scientific standards. We lack the perspective and the data to fashion a perfect literary image of the past. The product of the historian's craft is more like a painting than a photograph.

But if that is the case, then what is the purpose of writing and reading history? Barbara Tuchman argues that one should not place too much confidence in the "lessons of history." The reason for this caution, in her view, is that history is about humans, and human behavior is far from reliable.

> In human behavior and history it is impossible to isolate or repeat a given set of circumstances. Complex human acts cannot be either reproduced or deliberately imitated—or counted upon like phenomena of nature. The sun comes up every day. Tides are so obedient to schedule that a timetable for them can be printed like that for trains, though more reliable. In fact, tides and trains sharply illustrate my point: One depends upon the moon and is certain. The other depends upon man and is uncertain (1981:249).

If history cannot aid our predictions for the future, what can it do? Certainly it can help us understand and manage our present. But beyond this important use, history may be thought of as a moral art.

One must exercise extreme caution in any connection of the words *history* and *moral*. Early on in their college careers, budding historians learn that they may never use or abide the phrase *history proves*. The subjective aspect of the historian's craft renders the phrase impossible. Neophyte historians also are warned against moralizing from history. The American fondness for comparing the United States with the Roman Empire readily illustrates this historiographical sin. Certain problems are isolated, e.g., political corruption, runaway inflation, or sexual license, followed by a warning that the United States will suffer the same fate as the Roman Empire if these ills, whatever they might be, are not purged from the national life. This is historical moralizing, and it is a very great logical and historiographical fallacy.

When I suggest that history is a moral art, I hope that none of my readers will misinterpret me to be saying that I favor moralization. Rather, I mean that the writing and reading of history, the practice of it, ought to be political. It ought to be about our life together, whether in political, religious, or intellectual communities. This is to say further that the history that forms our communities is primarily a story, and thus that narrative is its proper form. Historical narrative is the historian's account of how we came to be the kind of people we are, whether people is to be understood as nation, church, political party, or the like. Embedded in that narrative will be accounts of what counted as virtues in any given period of our community's history. The presence of such virtues defines for us what a good community is. Also embedded in any honest historical narrative will be stories of our failures, mistakes, and even vices. Without this kind of truthfulness history becomes ideology, and its community loses the capacity for critical reflection upon itself.

To say that history is a moral art holds open the belief that historical narrative enables the moral development of persons who can critically reflect upon themselves and their communities. This narrative supplies conceptions of the good human being as conceived by the community it grounds. This narrative helps us to understand what we are to do as it grounds our self-awareness, for the community's narrative carries with it implications for our answer to the question, "Who is it that we are called upon to be?"

Certainly we are justified in concluding that narrative

performs important instrumental functions in the moral and political development of people. But can we make no stronger claims than to say that historical narrative is instrumentally useful? Hauerwas takes this line of thought a further step when he claims that narrative is intrinsic to the Christian church. He says, "There is no more fundamental way to talk of God than in a story."[7] Indeed "the very nature of Christian ethics is determined by the fact that Christian convictions take the form of a story, or perhaps better, a set of stories that constitutes a tradition, which in turn creates and forms a community" (1983:24). The stories and tradition to which Hauerwas refers are of course, the story of the people of God that begins in the opening pages of scripture and continues through Revelation. In a sense this story goes on through the centuries of Christian history down to our own day. If Hauerwas is correct, then at least concerning the Christian community, narrative is not only important as an instrument of our politics; it is our political art. Thus it is not only appropriate but critical to think of the church as an extended conversation about the meaning of its traditions, i.e., its narratives.

The writing and reading of historical narrative cannot be the province of a specialized minority of the community. Indeed the whole community ought to participate in the questioning conversation that is the moral and political outgrowth of the narrative: "What are the implications of this story for us?" "In light of this story, what are we called upon to be and do?" The narrative history that facilitates such questions is profoundly moral as it is simultaneously political.

III

Throughout this essay I have applied the term narrative to the product of the historian's activity. Some may be surprised to learn that such a move is controversial, but in fact it is. Less among historians than among some philosophers and literary critics there is a debate about the very idea of

153

narrative itself. The opposing sides of this debate range themselves on two sides of this question: Do human beings experience the events of their lives as a narrative composed of beginning, middle, and end, or are the events we experience actually random and therefore historians and novelists' narratives only a structure imposed on those random events to give coherence to that which is not really connected?

A leading exponent of the idea that narrative is a structure external to events is the literary critic, Hayden White. "Real events," claims White, "do not offer themselves as stories" (1987:4). Instead, he argues, historians give these events a narrative form. This "narrativizing discourse" serves an important cultural function and fills an apparently psychological need "not only to narrate but to give events an aspect of narrativity" (4).

According to White, before historical events were narrativized, they were presented in the form of annals or chronicles, lists of dates and important events. He contends that these historical lists lack cohesion. The events are presented as simply happening and the presentation makes no attempt to connect these events. What such lists lack "is a notion of a social center by which to locate them with respect to one another and to charge them with ethical or moral significance" (11). By the term "social center," White signifies approximately what I mean by the community. Thus White draws the closest possible relationship between narrative discourse and our polities. But there is this significant difference: White contends that communities, his "sociopolitical order" give rise to narratives, and I have stated the relationship conversely; narratives give rise to communities. White, borrowing from Hegel's understanding of the relationship between historicality, narrative, and law, cannot avoid the suspicion that narrative ultimately has to do with authority and power; i.e., the authority to construct, interpret, and tell the story rests in the hands of those who hold power. One cannot escape the inference that such power also confers the ability to narrativize events in a manner that legitimizes that power. Neither can one escape the conclusion that power has often been used in precisely this way; it would be foolish to deny that.

The view that I have ascribed to White has been challenged by Stephen Crites and Alasdair MacIntyre, among others. Essentially their arguments converge in the claim that narrative is not a structure but the inherently human experience of events. As MacIntyre says,

> Narrative form is neither disguise nor decoration. Humans are in their actions and practices, as well as their fictions, essentially storytelling creatures. [They] are not essentially, but become through their histories, tellers of stories that aspire to truth (1984:211-216 *passim*).

Stephen Crites also makes strong claims about the narrative quality of human experience (1971:291-311).[8] Whereas MacIntyre stresses narrative's relationship to community, Crites attempts to display the narrative quality of the individual's experience. He argues that the form of the experiencing consciousness is in some sense narrative. Furthermore, the narrative quality of its experience enables consciousness to mediate between the primeval stories in which consciousness rises and the narratives that consciousness constructs as explanatory accounts of the primeval. Even in this highly individualistic rendering of narrative experience, Crites acknowledges the communal dimension of experience.[9]

Debaters on either side of the argument about narrative share several ideas. They agree that narratives are extremely important to communities. They also share the idea that moral commitments are connected to narrative discourse. Their disagreements rise over the ontological question of the priority of narrative to politics.[10]

A famous Aristotelian metaphor might be employed here to illumine a possible point of convergence between the opponents in the narrative debate. Aristotle used the image of a flexible measuring tape to illustrate his insight into the interrelationship between rules and what he called "appearances," the matter-of-factness of our lives.[11] He observed that architects used a flexible tape in situations where a stiff measuring stick could not be applied. We all know the difficulty in using a wooden ruler to measure the circumference of a pipe. The shape of the pipe calls for a measuring instrument that possesses sufficient flexibility to permit its adaptation to the pipe. At the same time, the measuring instrument must possess sufficient "ruleness" and consistency that the pipe can be measured by an external standard. I am struck by the fact that narrative's champions and its structuralist critics both are partially right, and by the same token both are wrong. Narrative is a structure imposed on events but in the same sense as Aristotle's flexible measuring tape. Narrative does order events; it imposes this order on them as the tape imposes a measurement of inches or centimeters on a round pipe. But this order is not completely external to the events; it is not merely an external structure. For the narrative grows out of the events themselves. It can be told only as the events allow. Thus we may think of narrative as possessing elements of structure and flexibility.

The narrative debate raises fundamental epistemological questions that must be discussed. But that interesting project ranges too far afield of the scope of this essay. Here it is enough to say that both sides of the structuralist debate on narrative agree about its connections with politics and morality. If that is the case, then we might say that, insofar as the new history/old history debate is concerned, political history requires a narrative account and that account will have moral implications. Thus there is a particular kind of history, that which concerns our political or religious communities, which will necessarily require the form of narrative.

IV

The communities of which we are members, the nation or the church, are not storyless entities. They possess histories that shape their very characters. Moreover, these communities, insofar as they state expectations of their members, make narrative claims about the kind of people their members should be. The stories told by these communities tell of exemplary men and women who display the virtues valued by these communities and essential to their conception of a good human being. Storytelling is therefore among the most important moral and political arts of any community. Narrative history is one such form of storytelling.

Is the narration of a community's life the special province of an academically trained elite or the responsibility of an officially assigned "historian laureate?" Such questions must be answered mainly in the negative. Narrative history is a form of scholarship, and scholarship's rules must be followed. But the reading, writing and practice of history is not the privilege or the responsibility of a few. The production of the narratives that form our communities is an enterprise too power-laden to be entrusted to a minority.

The narratives of our communities must be accessible to all, in both the reading and writing of them. This broad accessibility is one of the few safeguards against the ideological corruption of history. When that corruption occurs, it is no longer possible for the prophet to call the community to account for having forsaken the narratives of its ancestors. Then history passes into ideology, and we lose the capacity to see ourselves as we really are, mired in our failures as well as exhilarated by our success. When we lose the ability to tell the truth about ourselves, our community loses the possibility of being true and good. For the community called the church, such an end means that we no longer can respond to the call to be God's people.

Fortunately, that bitter end does not need to be the fate of the people called the church. But to escape it we must constantly remember and, like the anonymous child of Deuteronomy 6, ask our parents to tell us the tale. For in it we will discover answers to the question, "What kind of people is God calling us to be?"

Chapter Seven Notes

1. Christians greatly fear the idea of politics in the church. Accuse people of "playing church politics" and you are asking for a fight. Thus we mistakenly believe that we must "keep politics out of the church," when what we really mean is to keep unfair or dirty politics out of the church. "Politics" simply is a way of being together. Unless a church or any other social organization wishes to disintegrate, it must have a way of being together. Thus the church ought not to avoid politics, but rather insure that its politics are in keeping with its witness as the people of God.

2. Aristotle, of course, concluded the *Nicomachean Ethics* with the resolve to turn this conversation about morals to the subject of politics. The various constitutions by which a polis might be organized had implications for the character of those city-states. St. Paul had much to say about believers' relationships with unbelievers, exhorting the former not to be unequally yoked with the latter. He also quoted a Greek moral maxim, "Bad company corrupts good morals," which Aristotle would have endorsed.

3. See especially Robert M. Bellah (1985) and Wade Clark Roof (1987).

4. See Stanley Hauerwas (1981:9-35); and Alasdair MacIntyre (1988:326-348).

5. Those interested in an analysis of this development and suggestions of the importance of virtue for moral philosophy should read Lawrence C. Becker (1975); for a strong argument that challenges dominant approaches to ethics and implicitly supports a virtue ethics see Edmund Pincoffs (1986). The neglected importance of the idea of virtue for Protestants is discussed in Eilert Herms, n.d. "Virtue."

6. Stanley Hauerwas (1981:35); Nancy Sherman's book *The Fabric of Character* (1989) includes an especially helpful discussion of the idea of character and vision from an Aristotelian point of view in the chapter "Discerning the Particulars."

7. Hauerwas (1983:25). For another illuminating discussion of the relationship of narrative to ethics, see McLendon (1986:328-256) "Why Narrative Ethics?"

8. (September 1971:291-311.) For a phenomenologically based argument that reaches similar conclusions about narrative and human experience, see David Carr (1986).

9. Janet Martin Soskice's fine study *Metaphor and Religious Language* (1985) raises the fruitful possibility of thinking of narrative as a metaphor. Soskice's account emphasizes the point that metaphor, far from being only figurative speech, in fact extends knowledge by speaking of one object in terms of another. Thus to think of narrative as a metaphor at least holds open the possibility of a way of construing narrative in a critical realist epistemology (as Soskice demonstrates) and yet retain White's appreciation of the fluidity of events. Narrative as metaphor, in other words is a way of thinking about narrative that may avoid the structuralist debate.

10. I am indebted to my colleague, Professor Fred Burnett, for this insight.

11. Martha C. Nussbaum explores the meaning of this metaphor in a chapter of her fine book *The Fragility of Goodness* (1986:290-317).

Bibliography

Barnes, Emily. 1898. *Gospel Trumpet.* 15 Aug.

Becker, Lawrence C. 1975. "The Neglect of Virtue." *Ethics* 85 (Jan) 2:110-122.

Bellah, et. al. 1985. *Habits of the Heart: Individualism and Commitment in American Life.* Berkeley: U Cal Pr.

Berry, R. L. 1927. "Can Any Good Come out of Lausanne? *Gospel Trumpet.* 14 July: Inside front cover.

Blewitt, C. J. 1925. "Stockholm Conference." *Gospel Trumpet.* 24 Sept:4-5.

Brookover, Opal F. 1908. "On Dress." *Gospel Trumpet.* n.d.

Brown, C. E. 1954. *When Souls Awaken.* Anderson, Ind: Gospel Trumpet Co.

———. n.d. *When the Trumpet Sounded.* Anderson, Ind: Warner Press.

———. 1945. *The Meaning of Sanctification.* Anderson, Ind: Warner Press.

Brown, Delwin. 1985. "Struggle til Daybreak: On the Nature of Authority in Theology. *Journal of Religion.* vol 65. no. 1:21.

Brueggemann, Walter. 1987. *Hope within History.* Atlanta: John Knox.

Burton, Rachel. 1984. *Gospel Trumpet.* 1 July.

Byrum, Enoch. n.d. *The Secret of Salvation.*

Byrum, Bessie. 1923. *Gospel Trumpet.* 29 Mar:7.

———. 1923. *Gospel Trumpet.* 1 Mar:13-14.

Byrum, Noah. n.d. *Familiar Names and Places.*

Byrum, R. R. 1925. *Christian Theology.* Anderson, Ind.: Gospel Trumpet Co.

Carr, David. 1986. *Time, Narrative and History.* Bloomington, Ind: Ind U Pr.

Crites, Stephen. 1971. "The Narrative Quality of Experience." *Journal of American Academy of Religion.* XXXIX (Sept) 3:291-311.

Gahmann, Lenora. 1904. "Whether to Be Led." *Den Evangeliske Basum.* 15 June:6.

Gray, A. F. 1946. *Christian Theology* vol. II. Anderson, Ind: Warner Pr.

Hatch, Nathan. 1989. *The Democratization of American Christianity.* New Haven: Yale U Pr.

Hauerwas, Stanley. 1986. "Authority and the Profession of Medicine." In *Suffering Presence: Theological Reflections on Medicine, the Mentally Handicapped, and the Church.* Notre Dame: U of Notre Dame Pr.

———. 1981. "The Significance of Vision: Toward an Aesthetic Ethics." In *Vision and Virtue.* Notre Dame, Ind: U of Notre Dame Pr.

———. 1983. *The Peaceable Kingdom.* Notre Dame, Ind: Univ. of Notre Dame Pr.

Henry, W. J. 1898. "The Evils of Tightlacing." *Gospel Trumpet* n.d.

Herms, Eilert. n.d. "Virtue: A Neglected Concept in Protestant Ethics." *Scottish Journal of Theology.* 35:481-495.

Hetrick, Gale. 1980. *Laughter among the Trumpets.* Lansing, Mich: Church of God in Michigan.

Himmelfarb, Gertrude. 1987. *The New History and the Old.* Cambridge: Harvard U Pr.

LeDeaut, Roger. 1971. "Apropos a Definition of Midrash." trans, by Mary C. Howard. *Interpretation.* XXV (July) 3:259-282.

Lindbeck, George. 1984. *The Nature of Doctrine: Religion and Theology in a Post-Liberal Age.* Philadelphia: Westminster.

Linn, Otto. n.d. *Studies in the New Testament.* vol. III. Anderson, Ind: Commercial Service.

Lopez, Amy. 1941. *Gospel Trumpet.* 26 Apr:7.

MacIntyre, Alasdair. 1984. 2nd ed. *After Virtue.* Notre Dame, Ind: U of Notre Dame Pr.

_____. 1988. *Whose Justice? Which Rationality?* Notre Dame, Ind: U of Notre Dame Pr.

Martin, Earl. 1942. *Toward Understanding God.* Anderson, Ind: Gospel Trumpet Co.

McLendon, James. 1986. *Ethics.* In *Systematic Theology* vol. I. Nashville: Abingdon.

Massey, James E. 1967. *Raymond A. Jackson: A Portrait.* n.p.

Mead, Sydney E. 1985. "The Rise of the Evangelical Conception of the Ministry." In *The Ministry in Historical Perspectives.* H. Richard Niebuhr and Daniel Day Williams, eds. San Francisco: Harper.

Moltmann, Jurgen. 1977. *The Church in the Power of the Spirit.* Translated by Margaret Kohl. New York: Harper.

Monroe, Warner. 1947. *An Introduction to Christian Ethics.* Anderson, Ind: Warner Pr.

Naylor, C. W. 1925. *God's Will and How to Know It.* Anderson, Ind: Gospel Trumpet Co.

_____. 1919. *Winning a Crown.* Anderson, Ind: Gospel Trumpet Co.

_____. 1922. *Heart Talks.* Anderson, Ind: Gospel Trumpet.

Neal, Hazel G. and Axchie A. Bolitho. 1982. rev. ed. *Madam President: The Story of Nora Hunter.* Anderson, Ind: Warner Pr, 1951.

Nelson, Thomas. 1908. *Home, Health and Success.* Anderson, Ind: Gospel Trumpet Co.

Nussbaum, Martha C. 1986. *The Fragility of Goodness.* New York: Cambridge U Pr.

Orr, C. E. 1903. *Christian Conduct.* Moundsville, Wv: Gospel Trumpet Co.

Pelikan, Jaroslav. 1985. *The Vindication of Tradition.* New Haven: Yale U Pr.

Phelps, J. W. 1912. *Gospel Trumpet.* 25 Apr:5-6.

Pincoffs, Edmund. 1986. "Quandary Ethics." In *Quandaries and Virtues.* Lawrence, Kans: U of KS Pubns.

161

Reardon, E. A. 1910. *Missionary Herald.* Nov:16.

Reardon, Robert. 1979. *The Early Morning Light.* Anderson, Ind: Warner Press.

Roof, Wade Clark and William McKinney 1987. *American Mainline Religion: Its Changing Shape and Fugure.* New Brunswick: Rutgers U Pr.

Sanders, James. 1984. *Canon and Community,* Philadelphia: Fortress Pr.

Shell, W. G. 1898. *Gospel Trumpet.* 24 Feb.

Sherman, Nancy. 1989. "Discerning the Particulars." In *The Fabric of Character.* New York: Oxford U Pr.

Simonsen, Micala. 1906. "Duty." *Den Evangeliske Basun (Gospel Trumpet).* 15 Dec:4.

Smith F. G. 1919. *The Last Reformation.* Anderson, Ind: Gospel Trumpet Co.

Smith, John W. V. 1985. *I Will Build My Church.* Anderson, Ind: Warner Press.

Smith, Sarah. n.d. *Life Sketches of Sarah Smith: A Mother in Israel.* Guthrie, Okla: Faith Pub. House.

Soskice, Janet Martin, 1985. *Metaphor and Religious Language.* Oxford: Clarendon Press.

Stafford, Gilbert. 1979. *Life of Salvation.* Anderson, Ind: Warner Pr.

Strege, Merle. D. 1991. "The Demise (?) of a Peace Church: The Church of God (Anderson), Pacificism and Civil Religion." *Mennonite Quarterly Review* Vol. XLV No. 2, (April) pp. 128-140.

Stevenson, Robert Louis. 1974. Qtd in *Catriona: The Further Adventures of David Balfour. Works* vol X. New York: AME Pr.

Tasker, George. 1924. Pamphlet, "An Appeal to the Free and Autonomous Churches of Christ in the Fellowship of the Evening Light." Calcutta, India:30.

Tasker, Mona Moors. 1979. Letter to Douglas E. Welch. 20 July.

Tuchman, Barbara W. 1981. *Practicing History.* New York: Knopf.

Tufts, Gorham. 1896. *Gospel Trumpet.* 19 Mar:3.

Warner, D. S., Joseph Fisher, and Allie Fisher. 1884. *Gospel Trumpet.* 1 August.

White, Hayden, 1987. *The Content of the Form: Narrative Discourse and Historical Representation.* Baltimore: Johns Hopkins U Pr.

Willimon, William. 1983. *The Service of God: How Worship and Ethics Are Related.* Nashville: Abingdon.

Yoder, John Howard. 1984. *The Priestly Kingdom: Social Ethics as Gospel.* Notre Dame, Ind: U of Notre Dame Pr.